Printed in the United States of America

First Printing, 2019

ISBN 9781700534934

A Girl Named Barrie, Inc.
www.agirlnamedbarrie.com

I dedicate this book to anyone who has dealt with infertility. And to Luca, my inspiration to make this world a kinder, better place.

Note: While this book is based in truth, some events have been altered for storytelling purposes. I don't go into every detail because there was SO MUCH. It should go without saying that this is just one person's story. No two infertile people will have the same path. If you think you are infertile, you can seek advice from your physician, a Reproductive Endocrinologist, or from reputable online ART resources like sart.org.

Trigger warning: This book talks about miscarriages.

I'm Infertile, How Are You?

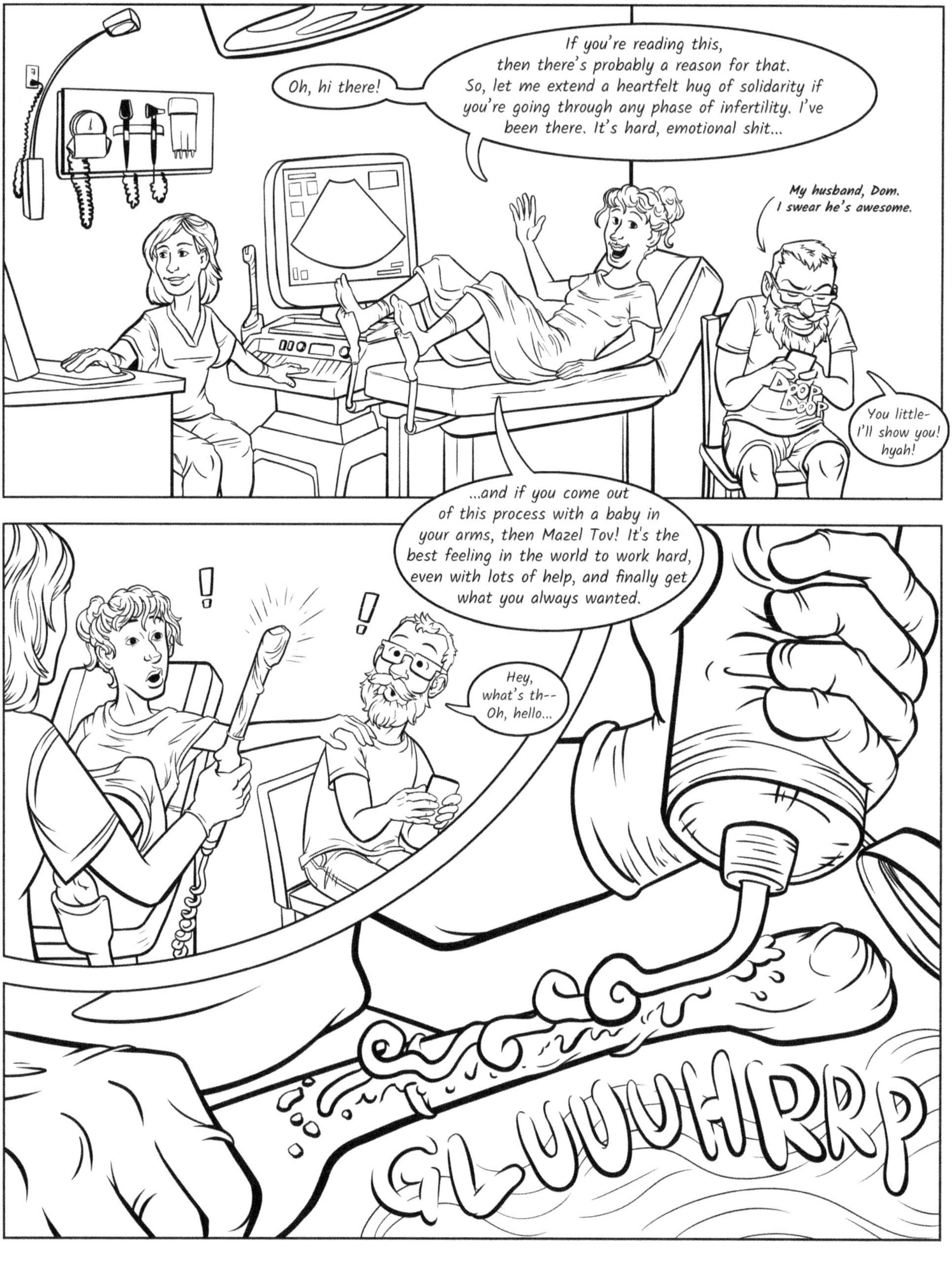
Oh, hi there!
If you're reading this, then there's probably a reason for that. So, let me extend a heartfelt hug of solidarity if you're going through any phase of infertility. I've been there. It's hard, emotional shit...
My husband, Dom. I swear he's awesome.
You little- I'll show you! hyah!
...and if you come out of this process with a baby in your arms, then Mazel Tov! It's the best feeling in the world to work hard, even with lots of help, and finally get what you always wanted.
Hey, what's th-- Oh, hello...
GLUUUHRRP

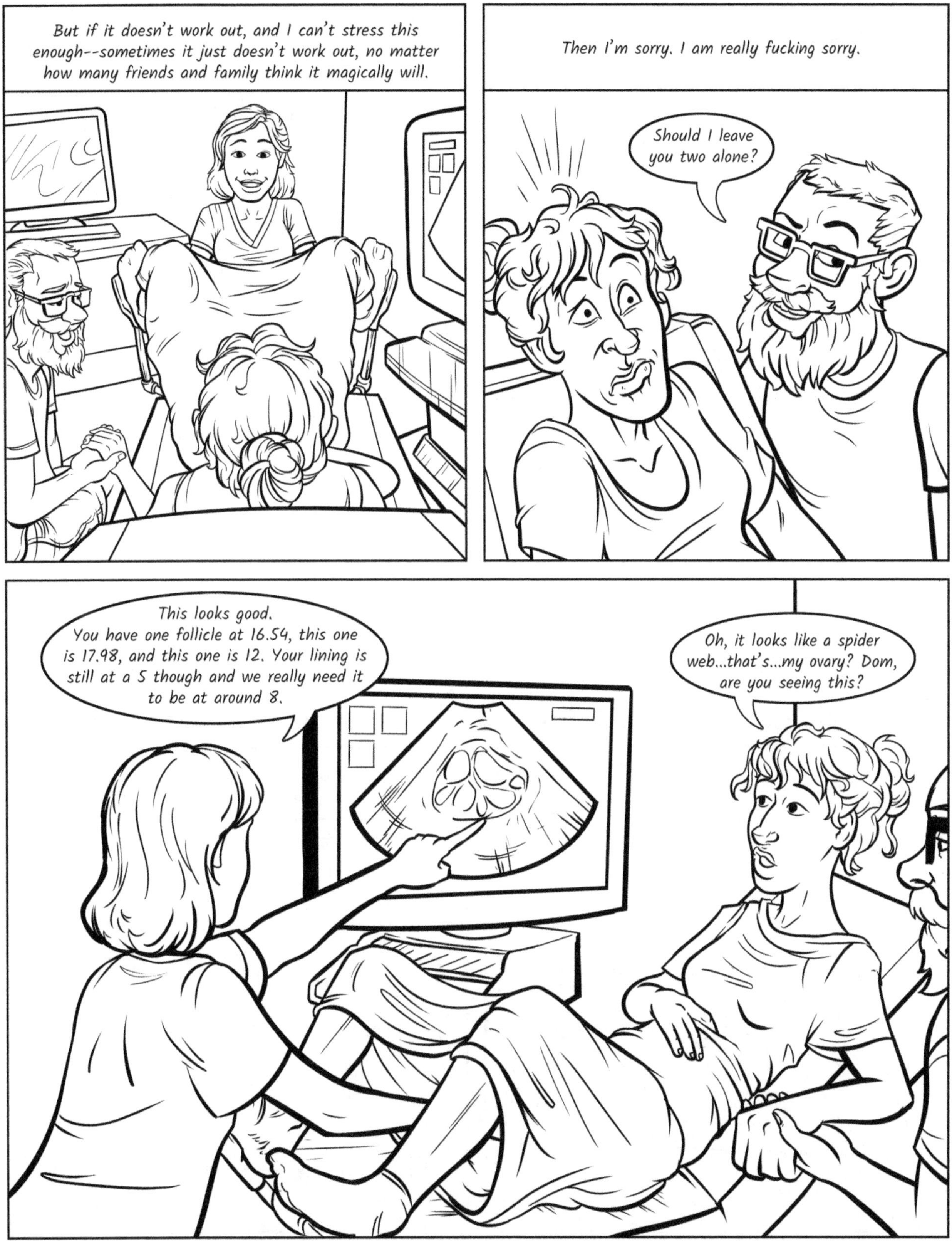
But if it doesn't work out, and I can't stress this enough--sometimes it just doesn't work out, no matter how many friends and family think it magically will.
Then I'm sorry. I am really fucking sorry.
Should I leave you two alone?
This looks good. You have one follicle at 16.54, this one is 17.98, and this one is 12. Your lining is still at a 5 though and we really need it to be at around 8.
Oh, it looks like a spider web...that's...my ovary? Dom, are you seeing this?

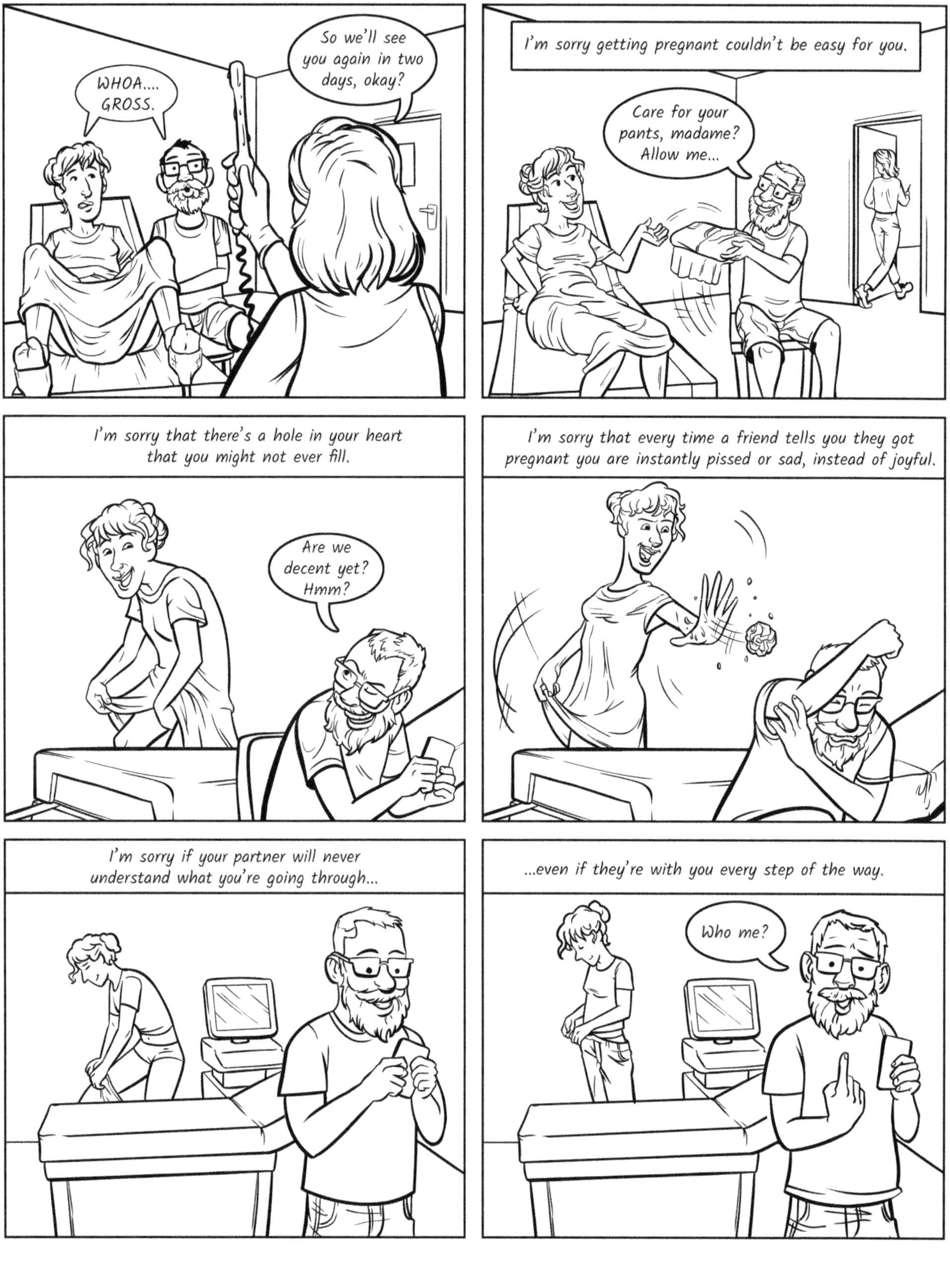
WHOA.... GROSS.
So we'll see you again in two days, okay?
I'm sorry getting pregnant couldn't be easy for you.
Care for your pants, madame? Allow me...
I'm sorry that there's a hole in your heart that you might not ever fill.
Are we decent yet? Hmm?
I'm sorry that every time a friend tells you they got pregnant you are instantly pissed or sad, instead of joyful.
I'm sorry if your partner will never understand what you're going through...
...even if they're with you every step of the way.
Who me?

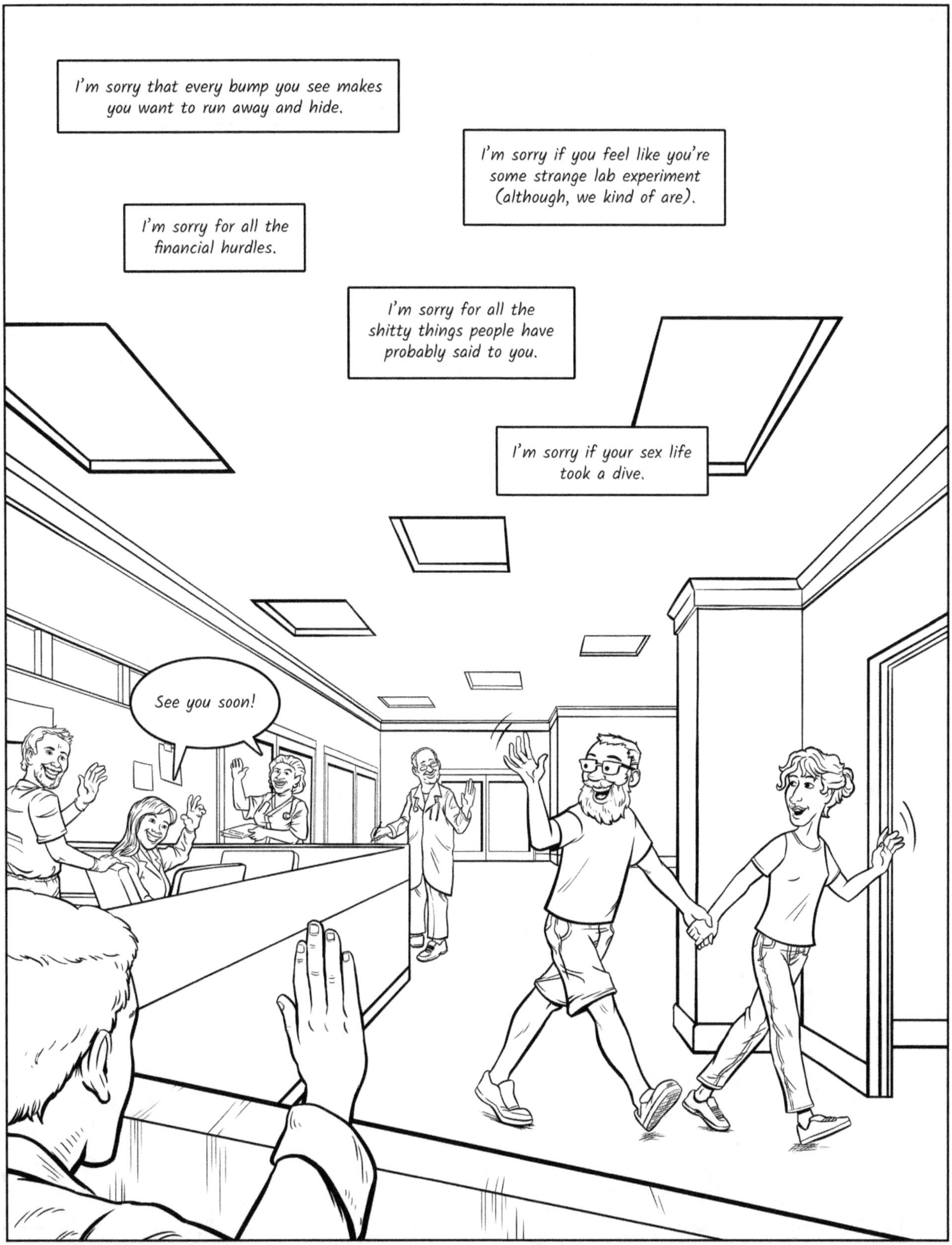
I'm sorry that every bump you see makes you want to run away and hide.
I'm sorry if you feel like you're some strange lab experiment (although, we kind of are).
I'm sorry for all the financial hurdles.
I'm sorry for all the shitty things people have probably said to you.
I'm sorry if your sex life took a dive.
See you soon!

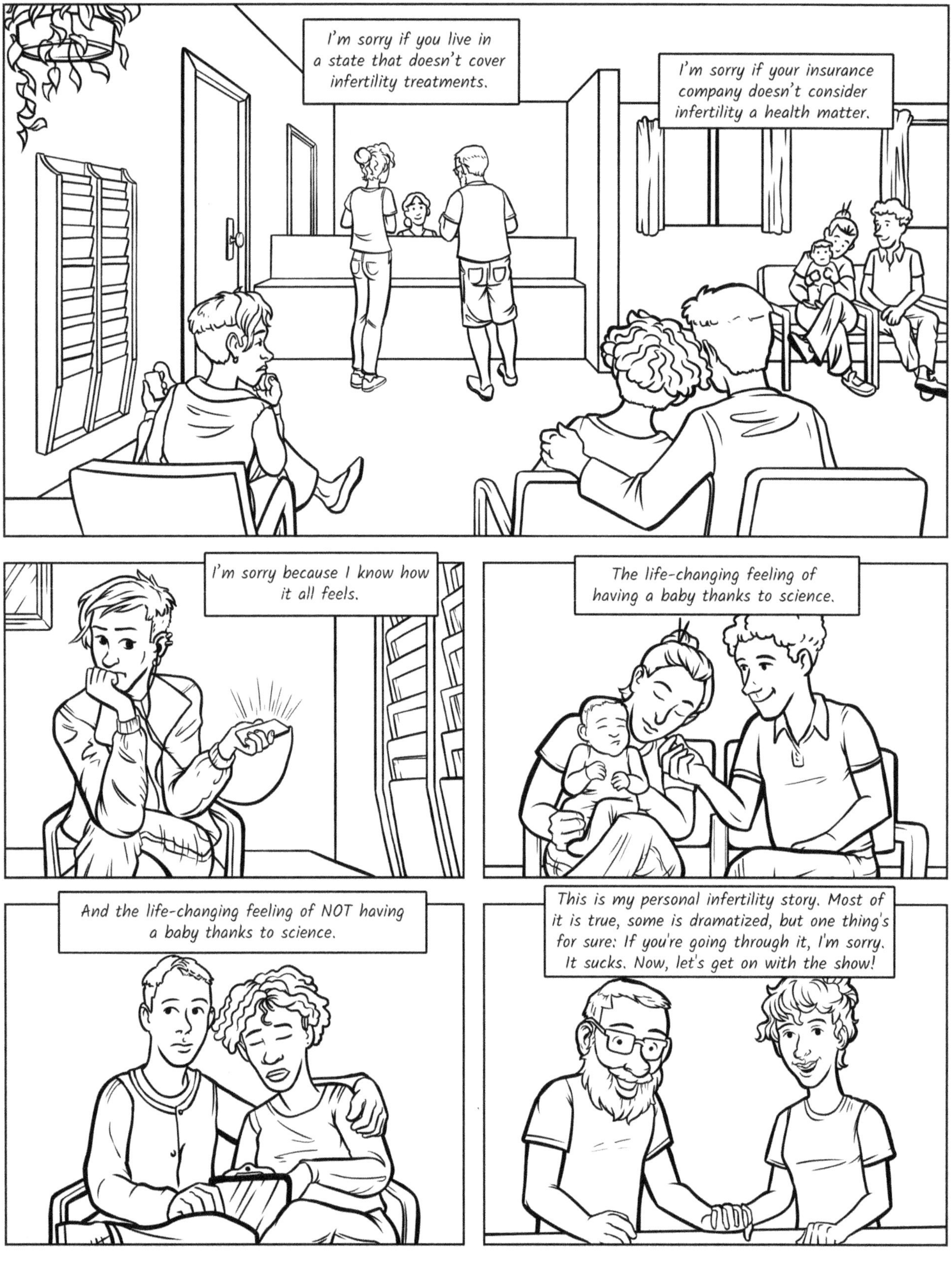
I'm sorry if you live in a state that doesn't cover infertility treatments.
I'm sorry if your insurance company doesn't consider infertility a health matter.
I'm sorry because I know how it all feels.
The life-changing feeling of having a baby thanks to science.
And the life-changing feeling of NOT having a baby thanks to science.
This is my personal infertility story. Most of it is true, some is dramatized, but one thing's for sure: If you're going through it, I'm sorry. It sucks. Now, let's get on with the show!

Acronyms & Definitions

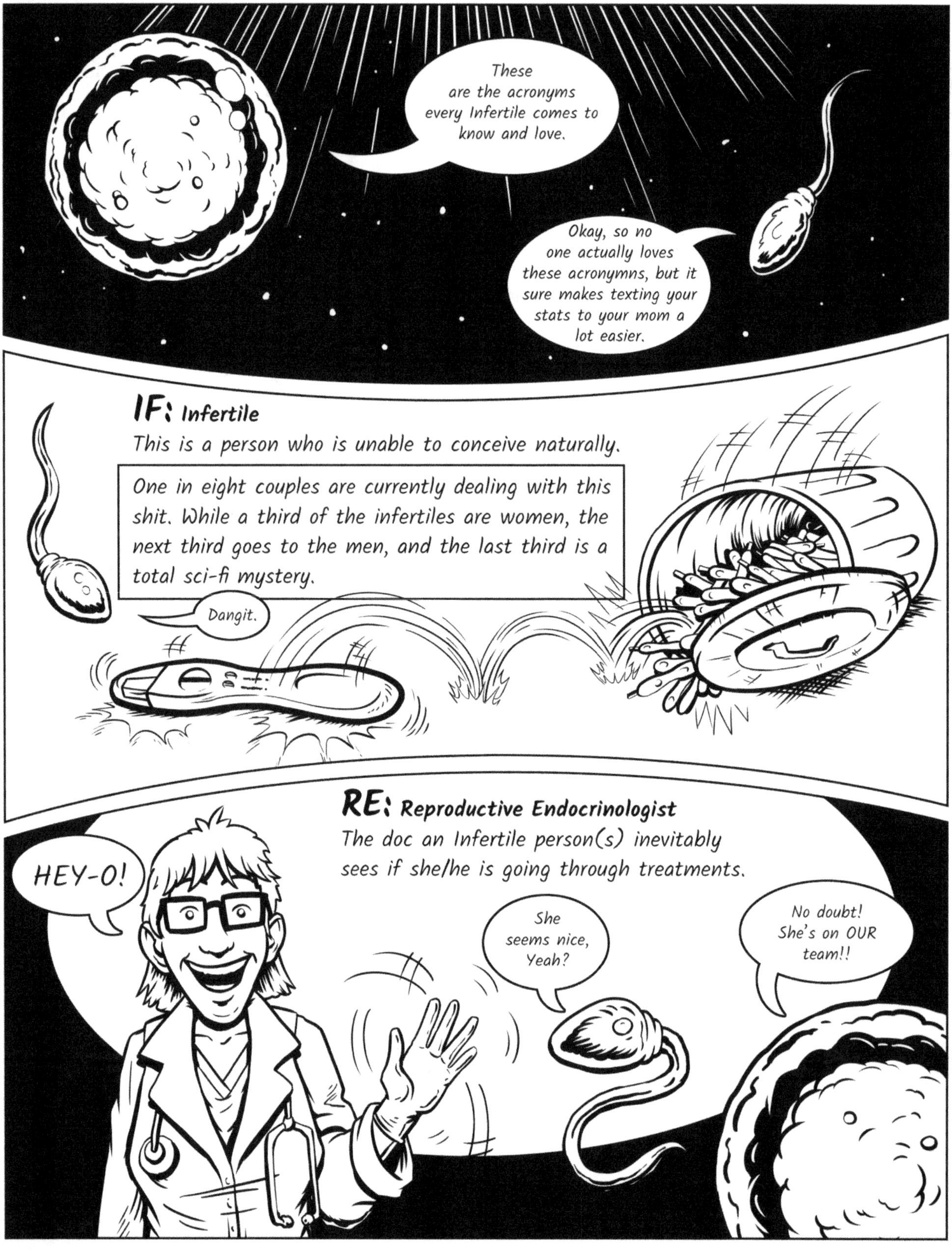
These are the acronyms every Infertile comes to know and love.
Okay, so no one actually loves these acronymns, but it sure makes texting your stats to your mom a lot easier.
IF: Infertile
This is a person who is unable to conceive naturally.
One in eight couples are currently dealing with this shit. While a third of the infertiles are women, the next third goes to the men, and the last third is a total sci-fi mystery.
Dangit.
RE: Reproductive Endocrinologist
The doc an Infertile person(s) inevitably sees if she/he is going through treatments.
HEY-O!
She seems nice, Yeah?
No doubt! She's on OUR team!!

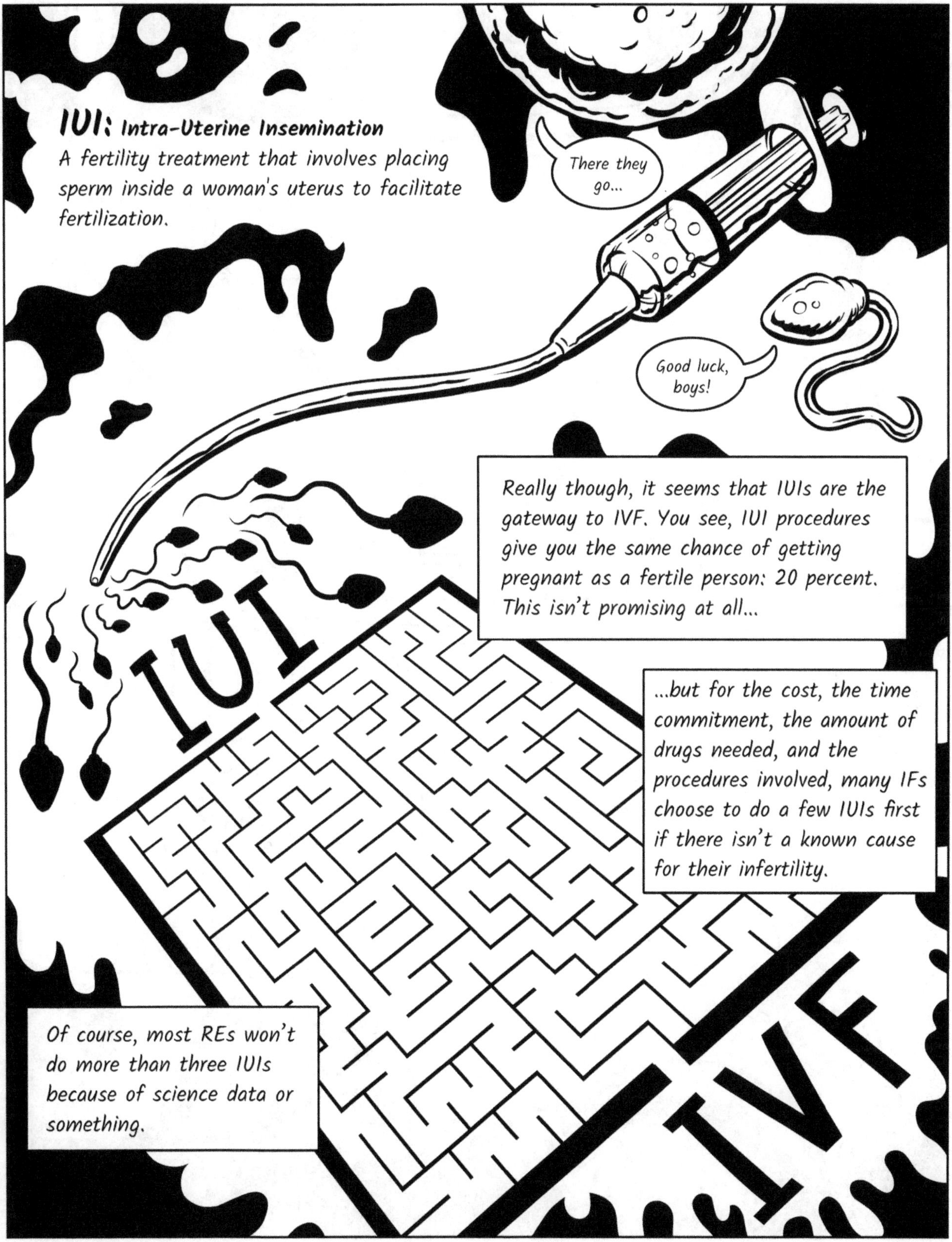
IUI: Intra-Uterine Insemination
A fertility treatment that involves placing sperm inside a woman's uterus to facilitate fertilization.
There they go...
Good luck, boys!
Really though, it seems that IUIs are the gateway to IVF. You see, IUI procedures give you the same chance of getting pregnant as a fertile person: 20 percent. This isn't promising at all...
IUI
...but for the cost, the time commitment, the amount of drugs needed, and the procedures involved, many IFs choose to do a few IUIs first if there isn't a known cause for their infertility.
IVF
Of course, most REs won't do more than three IUIs because of science data or something.

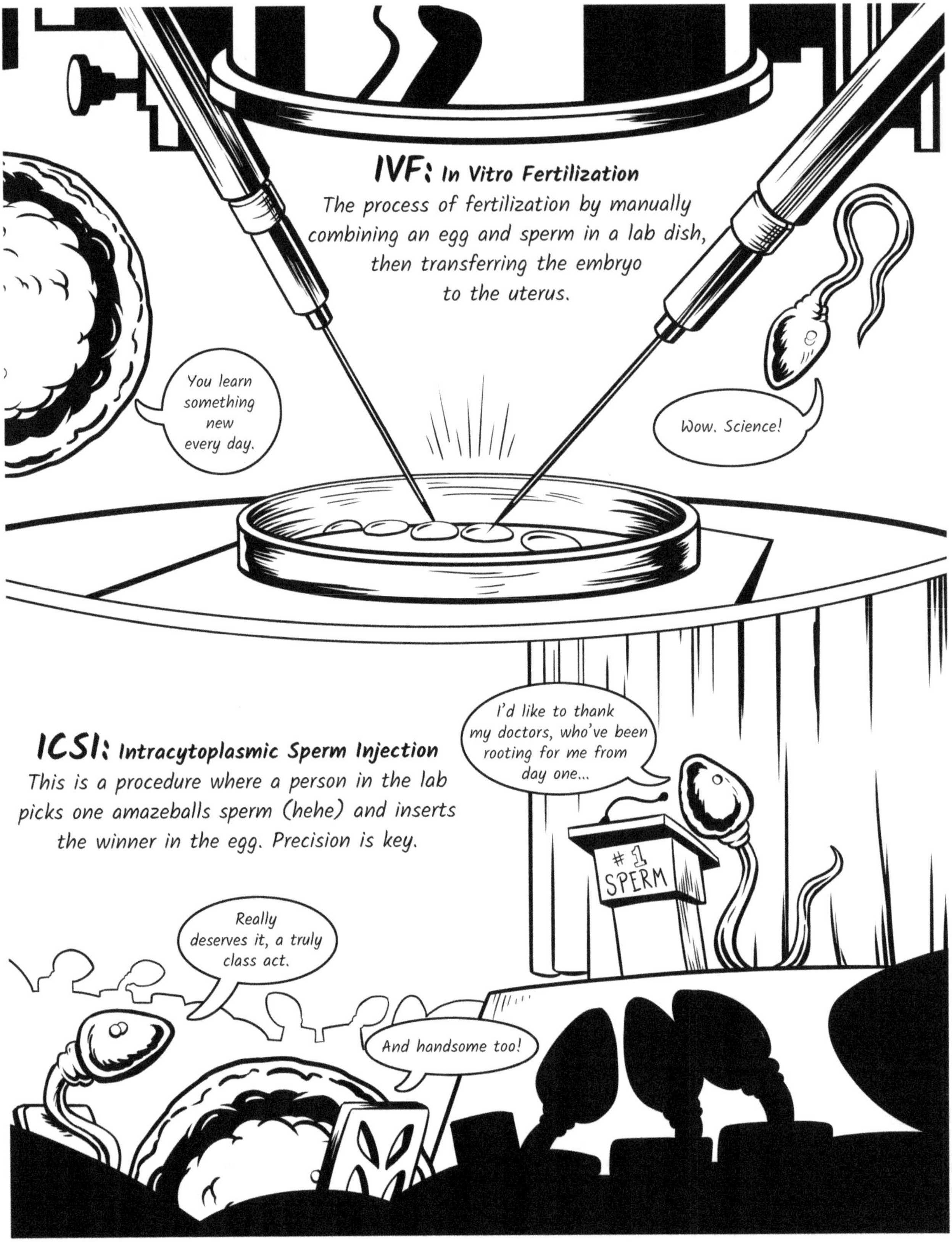
IVF: In Vitro Fertilization
The process of fertilization by manually combining an egg and sperm in a lab dish, then transferring the embryo to the uterus.
You learn something new every day.
Wow. Science!
ICSI: Intracytoplasmic Sperm Injection
This is a procedure where a person in the lab picks one amazeballs sperm (hehe) and inserts the winner in the egg. Precision is key.
I'd like to thank my doctors, who've been rooting for me from day one...
#1 SPERM
Really deserves it, a truly class act.
And handsome too!

FET: Frozen Egg Transfer

Once the IVF lab stuff is done and the blastocyst (an embryo made of about 100 cells) properly plumps up, it's frozen so the lady can be primed for the "perfect" transfer.

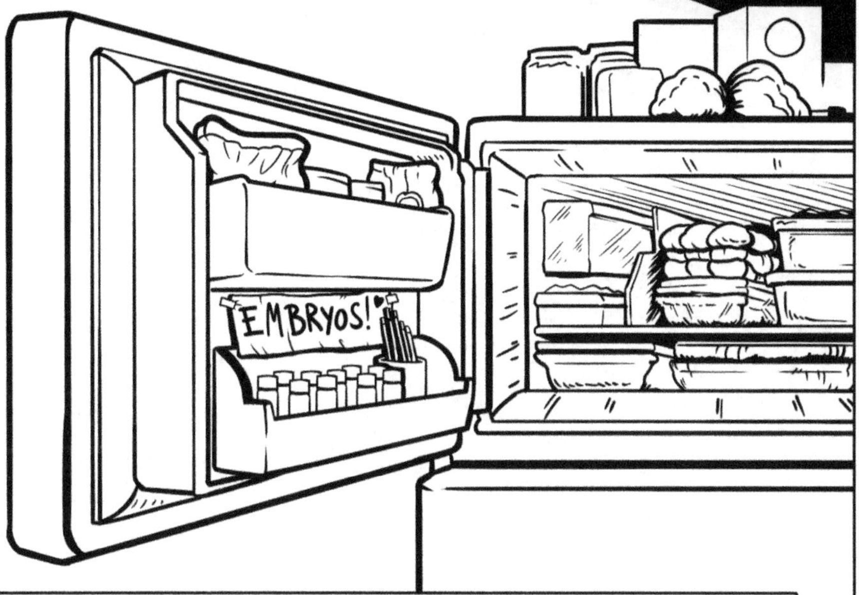
EMBRYOS!

Some people prefer fresh transfers because it's a faster process, it's probably cheaper, and doesn't require the extensive amount of drugs since you do it soon after retrieving the eggs. Others prefer an FET because they get a welcome break between retrieval and transfer.

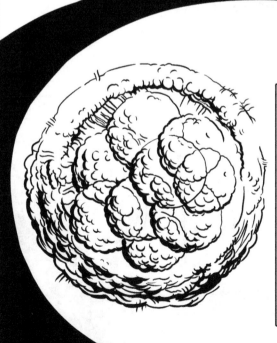

PUPO: Pregnant Until Proven Otherwise

A term IFs use after they've been implanted with an embryo (sperm + egg).

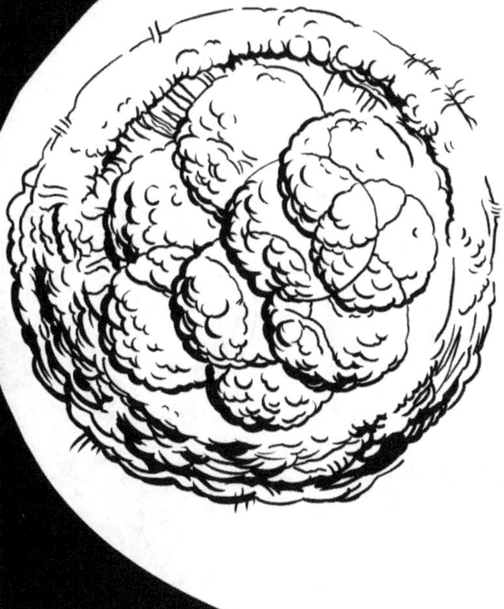

Since IVF procedures usually implant a three or five day old embryo (aka: blastocyst, aka: the beginnings of a baby), you are technically considered pregnant until you take a pregnancy test and a couple of blood tests.

This is a HUGE, cautiously optimistic time in an IF's journey and they've been wishing on every magical stone given to them by their Reiki healer just to use this funny sounding acronym. If anyone gets to say they're PUPO they deserve a Carvel cake with the whale on it and everything.

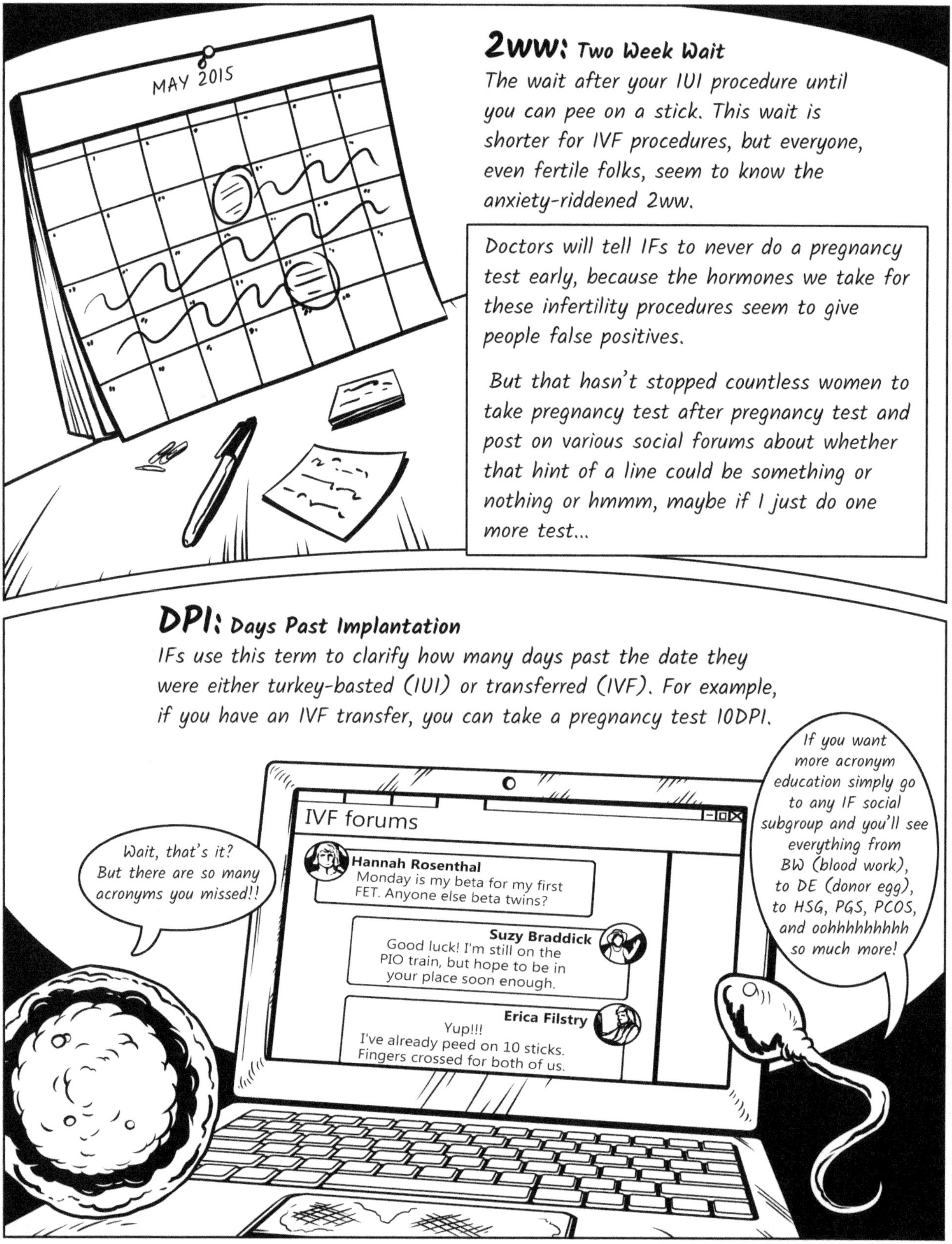
MAY 2015
2ww: Two Week Wait
The wait after your IUI procedure until you can pee on a stick. This wait is shorter for IVF procedures, but everyone, even fertile folks, seem to know the anxiety-riddened 2ww.
Doctors will tell IFs to never do a pregnancy test early, because the hormones we take for these infertility procedures seem to give people false positives.
But that hasn't stopped countless women to take pregnancy test after pregnancy test and post on various social forums about whether that hint of a line could be something or nothing or hmmm, maybe if I just do one more test...
DPI: Days Past Implantation
IFs use this term to clarify how many days past the date they were either turkey-basted (IUI) or transferred (IVF). For example, if you have an IVF transfer, you can take a pregnancy test 10DPI.
Wait, that's it? But there are so many acronyms you missed!!
IVF forums
Hannah Rosenthal
Monday is my beta for my first FET. Anyone else beta twins?
Suzy Braddick
Good luck! I'm still on the PIO train, but hope to be in your place soon enough.
Erica Filstry
Yup!!! I've already peed on 10 sticks. Fingers crossed for both of us.
If you want more acronym education simply go to any IF social subgroup and you'll see everything from BW (blood work), to DE (donor egg), to HSG, PGS, PCOS, and oohhhhhhhhhh so much more!

My Gateway To IVF

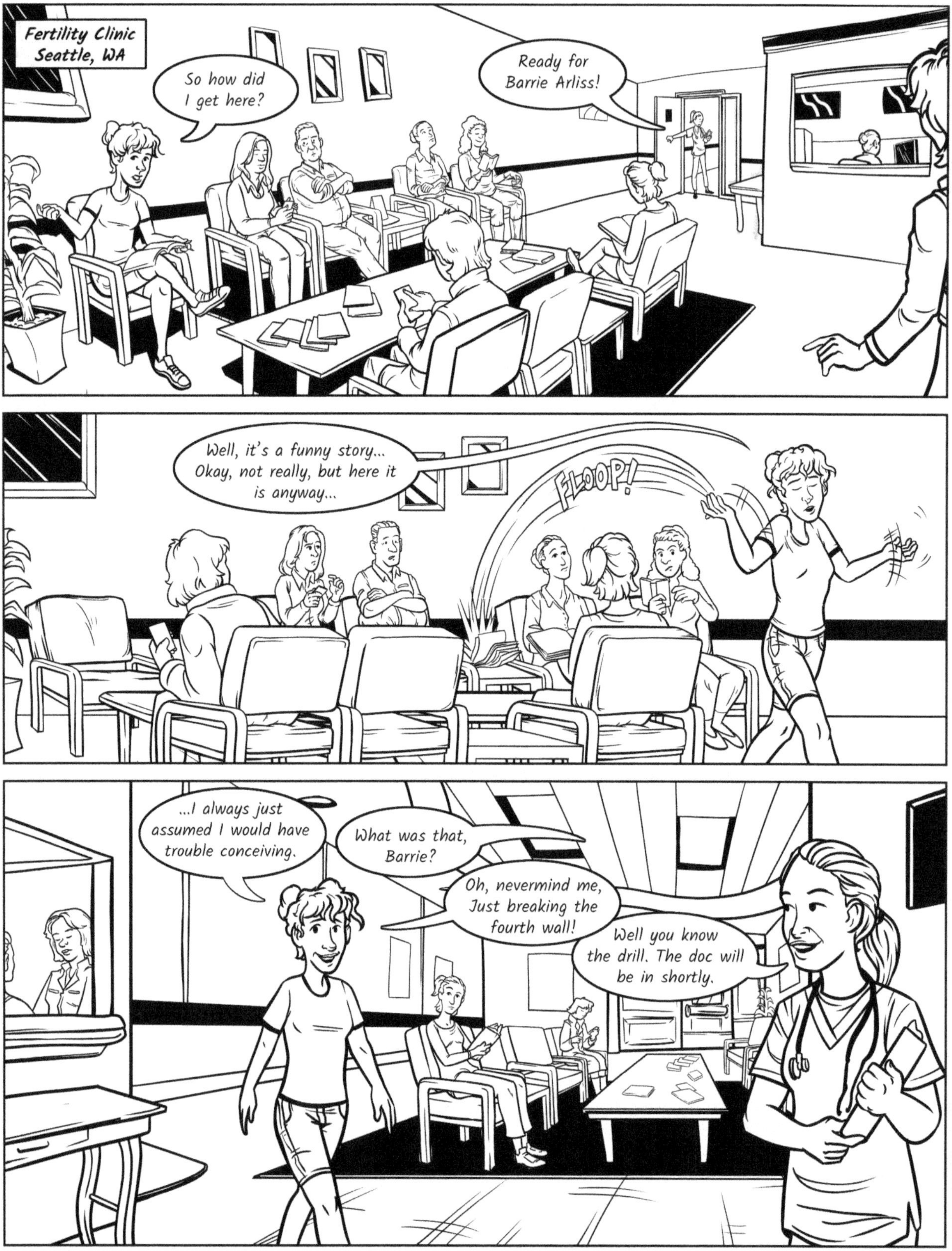
Fertility Clinic Seattle, WA
So how did I get here?
Ready for Barrie Arliss!
Well, it's a funny story... Okay, not really, but here it is anyway...
FLOOP!
...I always just assumed I would have trouble conceiving.
What was that, Barrie?
Oh, nevermind me, Just breaking the fourth wall!
Well you know the drill. The doc will be in shortly.

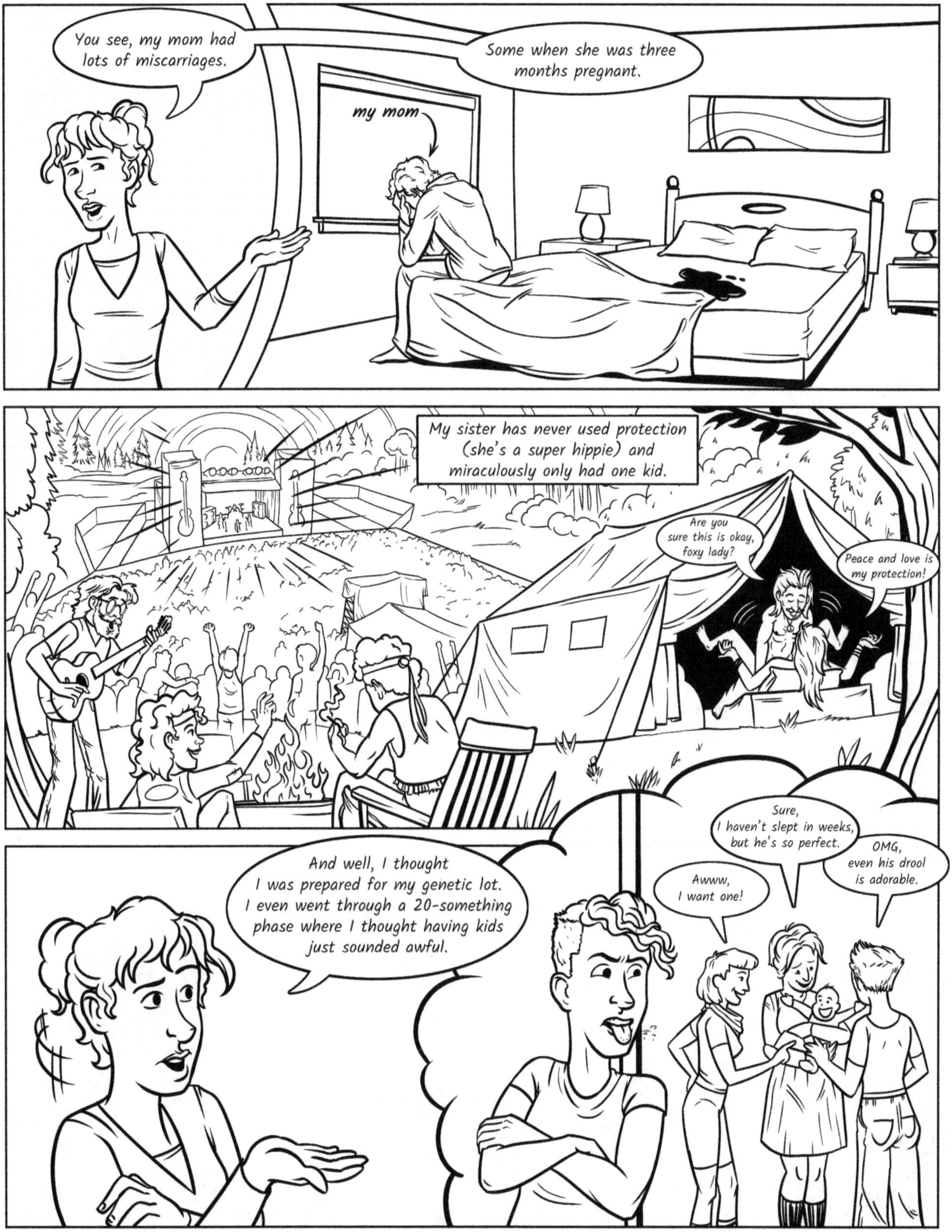
You see, my mom had lots of miscarriages.
Some when she was three months pregnant.
my mom
My sister has never used protection (she's a super hippie) and miraculously only had one kid.
Are you sure this is okay, foxy lady?
Peace and love is my protection!
And well, I thought I was prepared for my genetic lot. I even went through a 20-something phase where I thought having kids just sounded awful.
Awww, I want one!
Sure, I haven't slept in weeks, but he's so perfect.
OMG, even his drool is adorable.

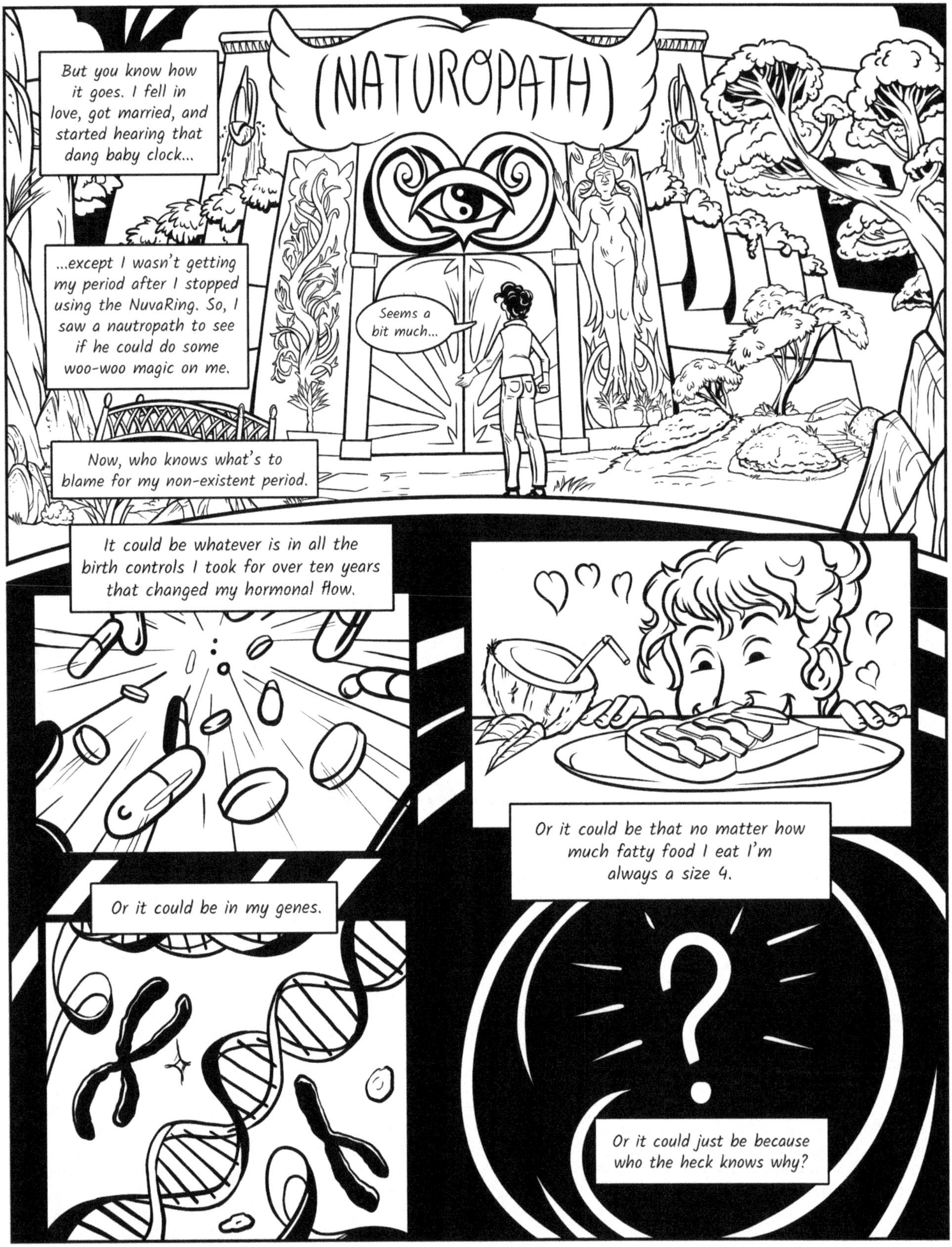
NATUROPATH
But you know how it goes. I fell in love, got married, and started hearing that dang baby clock...
...except I wasn't getting my period after I stopped using the NuvaRing. So, I saw a nautropath to see if he could do some woo-woo magic on me.
Seems a bit much...
Now, who knows what's to blame for my non-existent period.
It could be whatever is in all the birth controls I took for over ten years that changed my hormonal flow.
Or it could be that no matter how much fatty food I eat I'm always a size 4.
Or it could be in my genes.
Or it could just be because who the heck knows why?

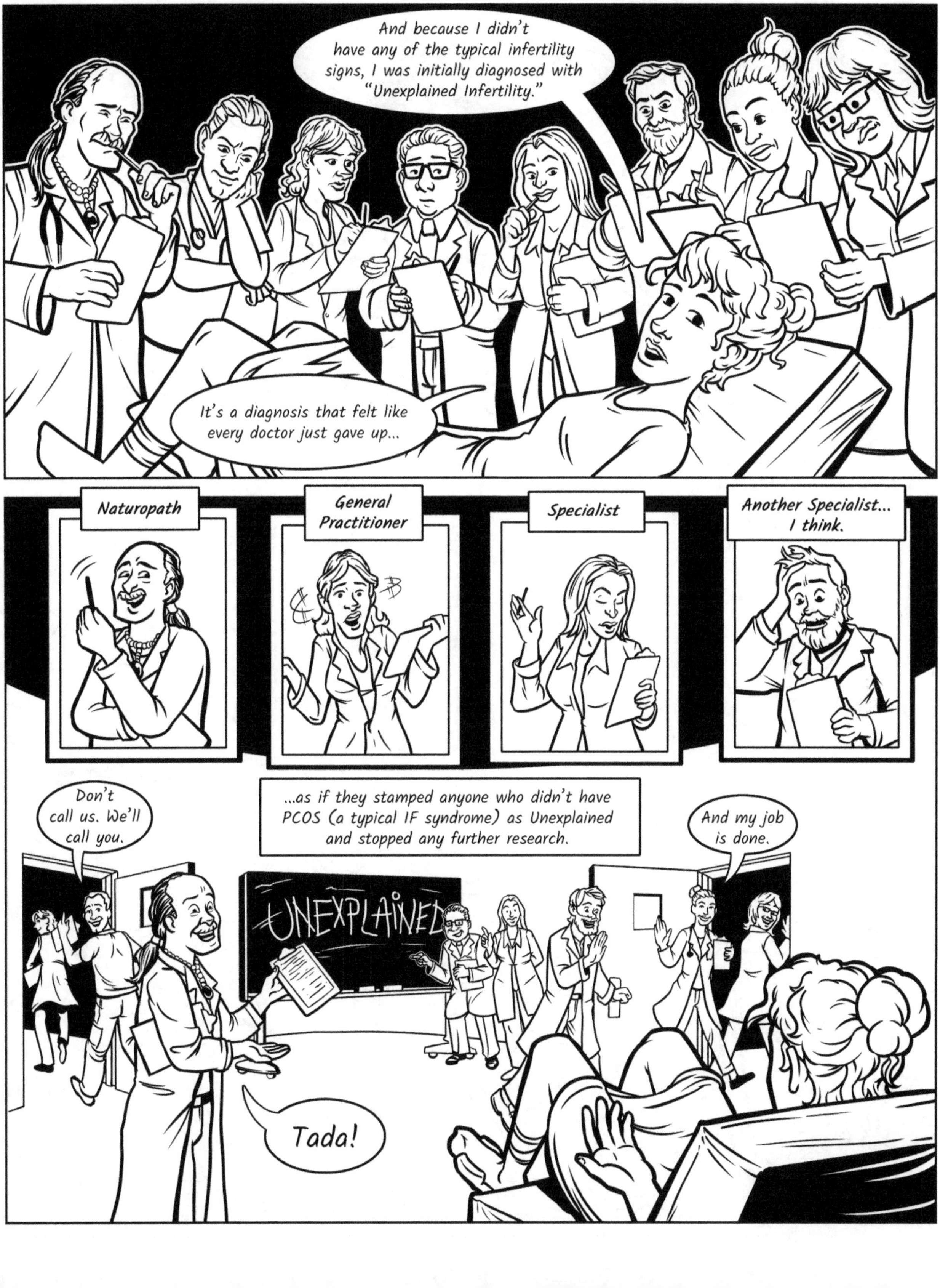

And because I didn't have any of the typical infertility signs, I was initially diagnosed with "Unexplained Infertility."
It's a diagnosis that felt like every doctor just gave up...
Naturopath
General Practitioner
Specialist
Another Specialist... I think.
...as if they stamped anyone who didn't have PCOS (a typical IF syndrome) as Unexplained and stopped any further research.
Don't call us. We'll call you.
And my job is done.
UNEXPLAINED
Tada!

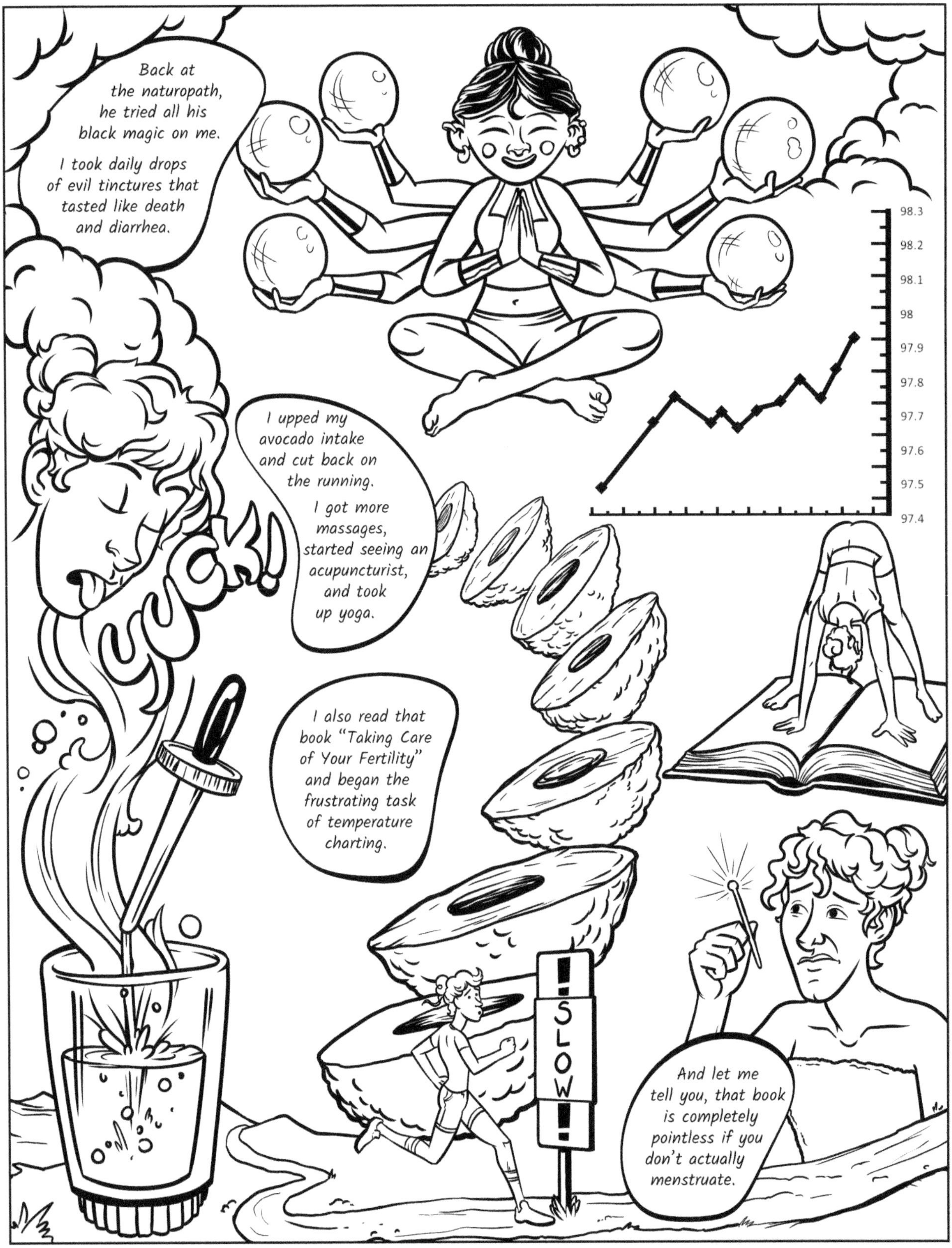
Back at the naturopath, he tried all his black magic on me.
I took daily drops of evil tinctures that tasted like death and diarrhea.
98.3
98.2
98.1
98
97.9
97.8
97.7
97.6
97.5
97.4
I upped my avocado intake and cut back on the running.
I got more massages, started seeing an acupuncturist, and took up yoga.
YUCK!
I also read that book "Taking Care of Your Fertility" and began the frustrating task of temperature charting.
SLOW
And let me tell you, that book is completely pointless if you don't actually menstruate.

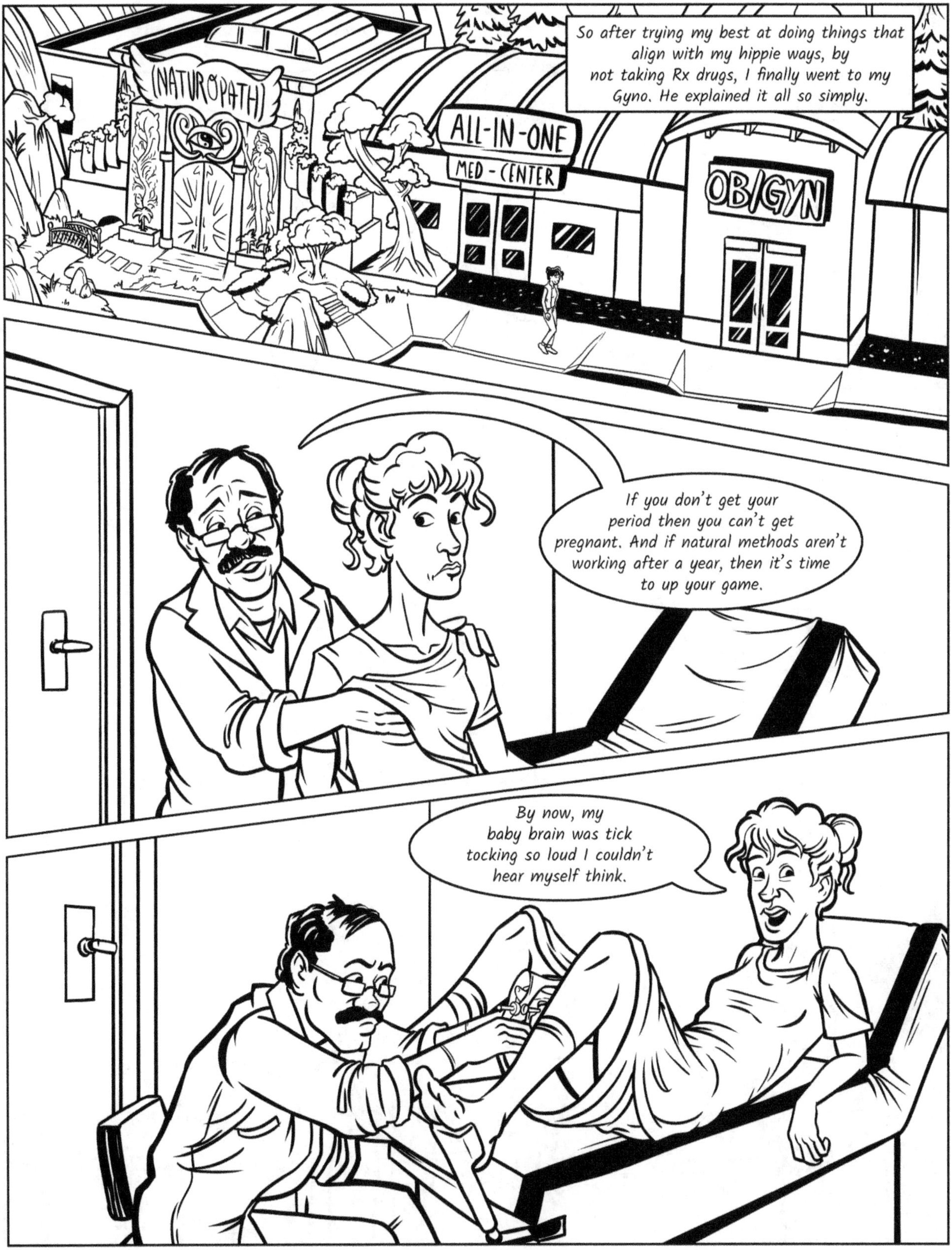
NATUROPATH
ALL-IN-ONE
MED-CENTER
OB/GYN
So after trying my best at doing things that align with my hippie ways, by not taking Rx drugs, I finally went to my Gyno. He explained it all so simply.
If you don't get your period then you can't get pregnant. And if natural methods aren't working after a year, then it's time to up your game.
By now, my baby brain was tick tocking so loud I couldn't hear myself think.

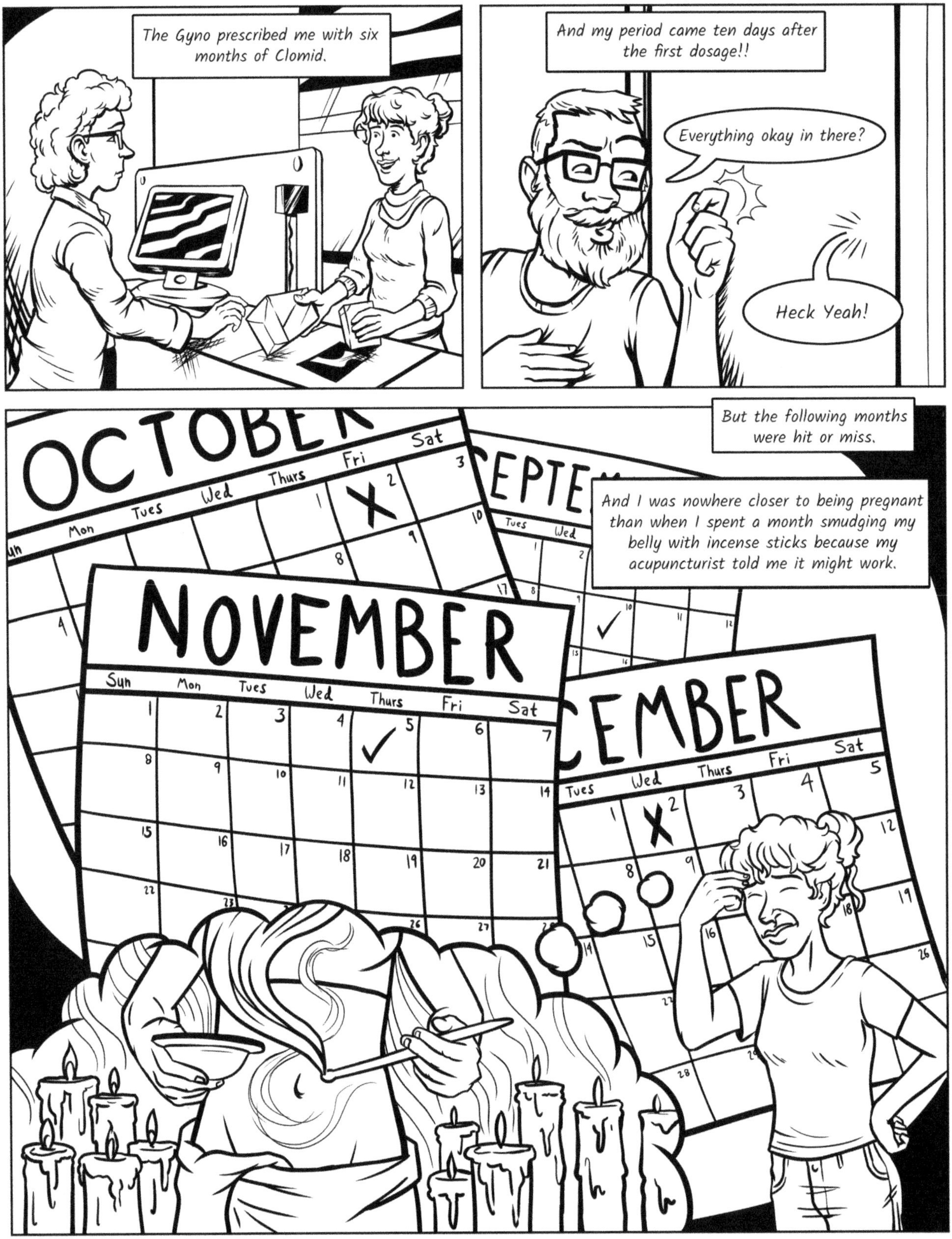

The Gyno prescribed me with six months of Clomid.
And my period came ten days after the first dosage!!
Everything okay in there?
Heck Yeah!
But the following months were hit or miss.
And I was nowhere closer to being pregnant than when I spent a month smudging my belly with incense sticks because my acupuncturist told me it might work.
OCTOBER
NOVEMBER
CEMBER

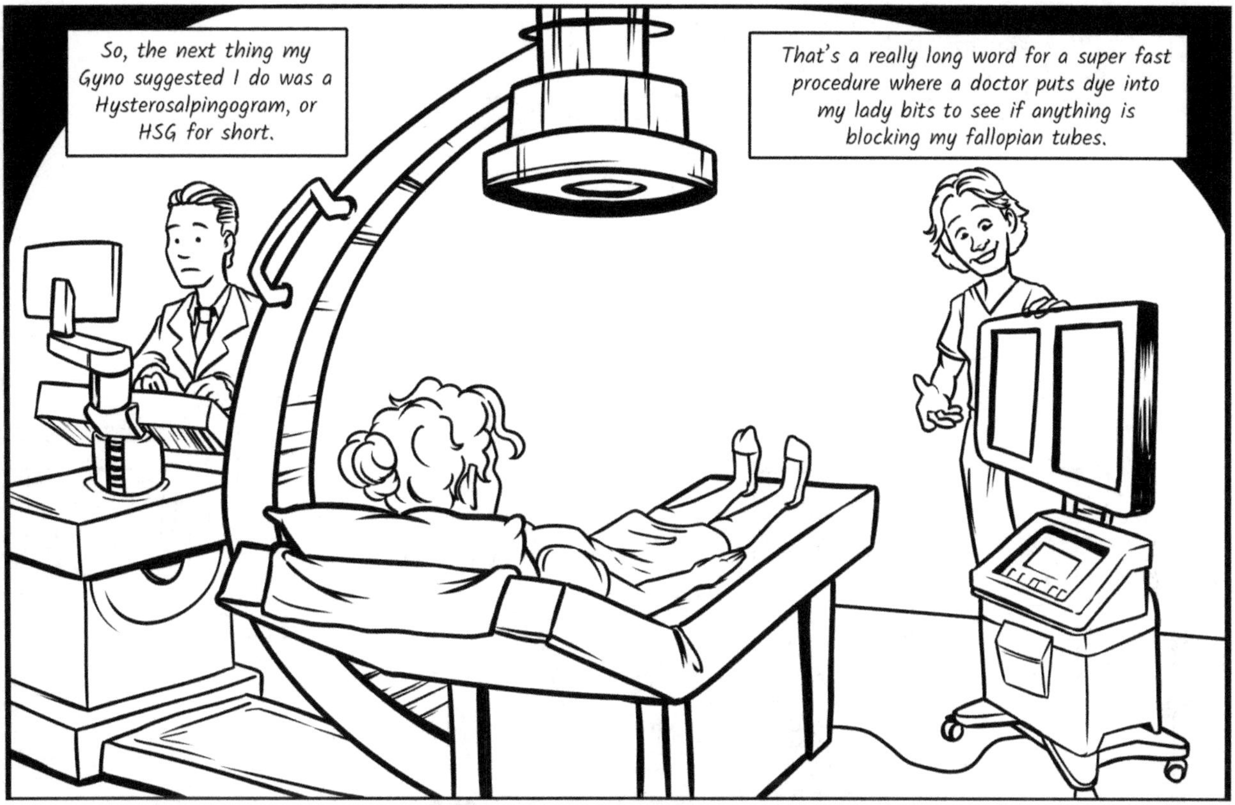
So, the next thing my Gyno suggested I do was a Hysterosalpingogram, or HSG for short.
That's a really long word for a super fast procedure where a doctor puts dye into my lady bits to see if anything is blocking my fallopian tubes.

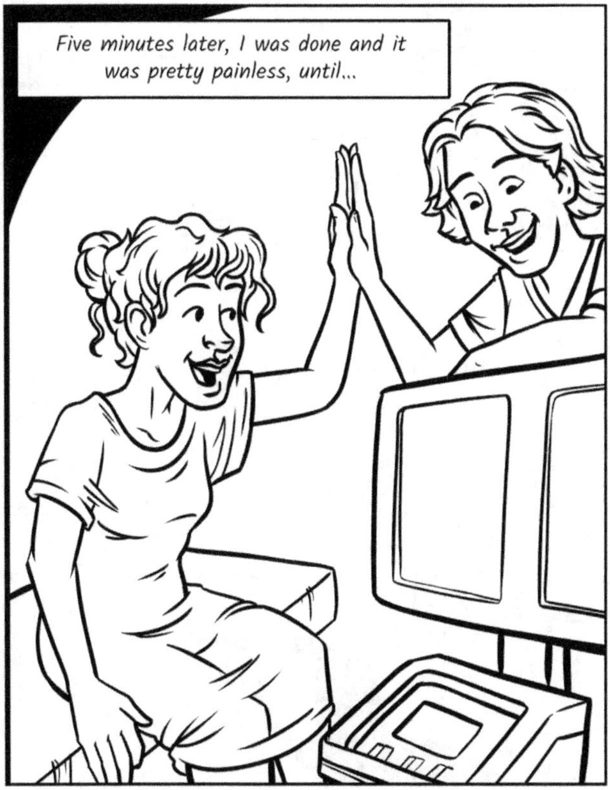
Five minutes later, I was done and it was pretty painless, until...

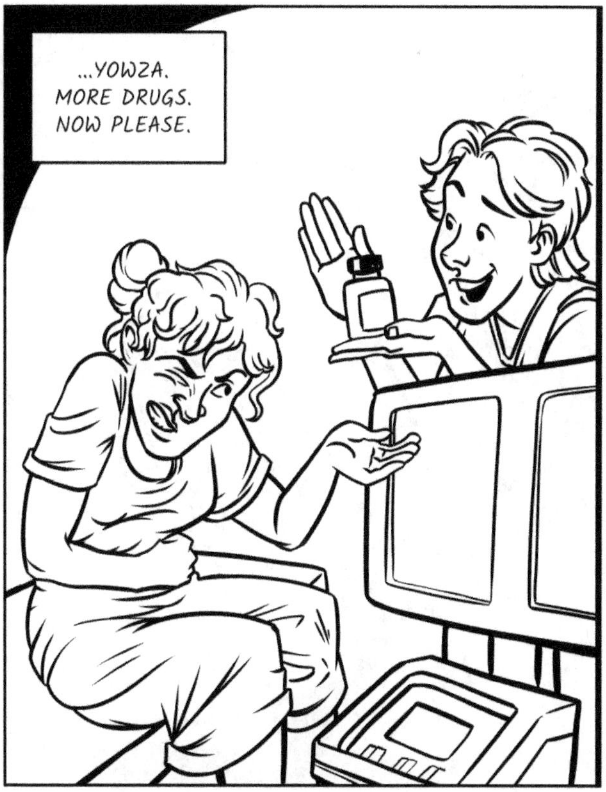
...YOWZA.
MORE DRUGS.
NOW PLEASE.

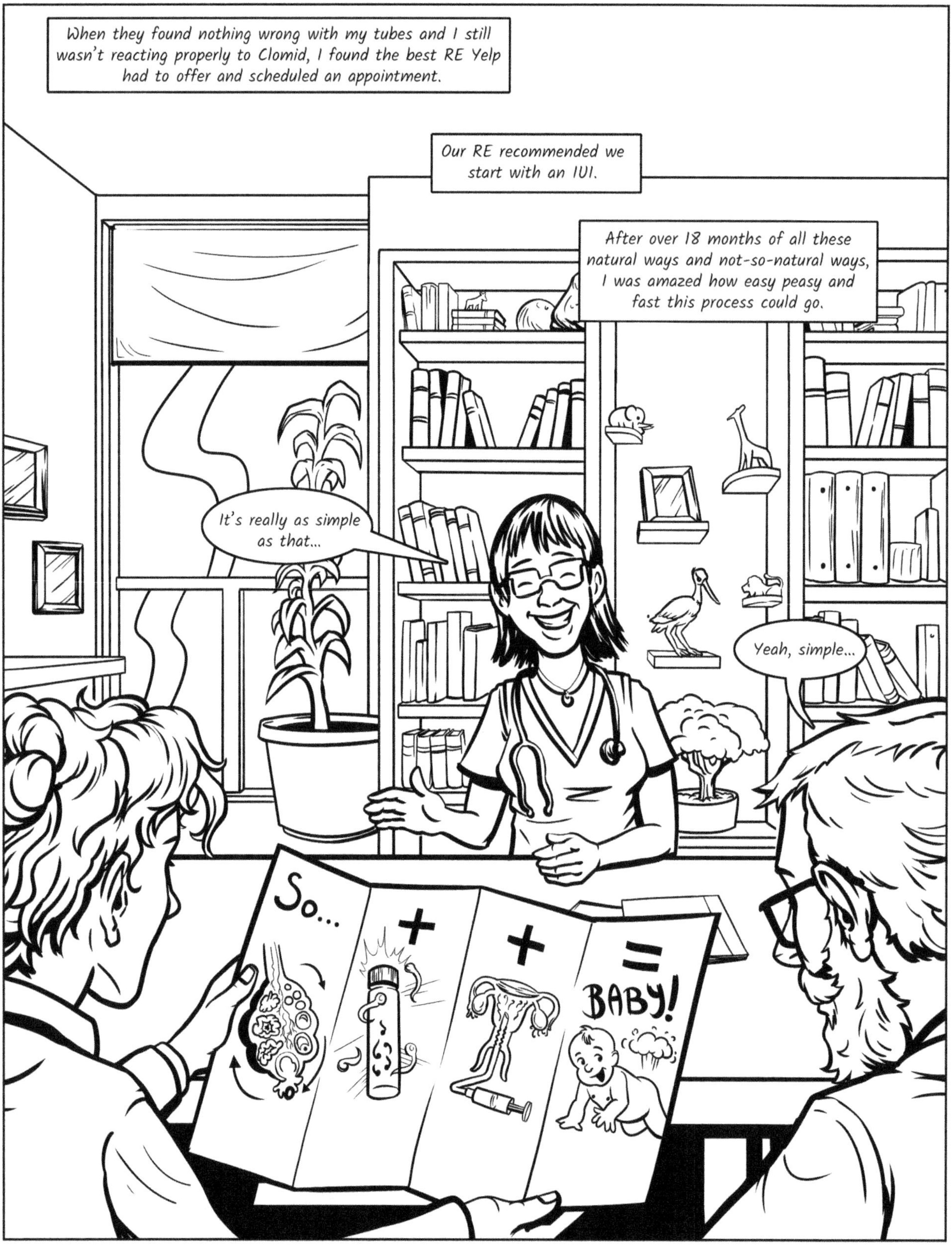
When they found nothing wrong with my tubes and I still wasn't reacting properly to Clomid, I found the best RE Yelp had to offer and scheduled an appointment.
Our RE recommended we start with an IUI.
After over 18 months of all these natural ways and not-so-natural ways, I was amazed how easy peasy and fast this process could go.
It's really as simple as that...
Yeah, simple...
So...
+
+
=
BABY!

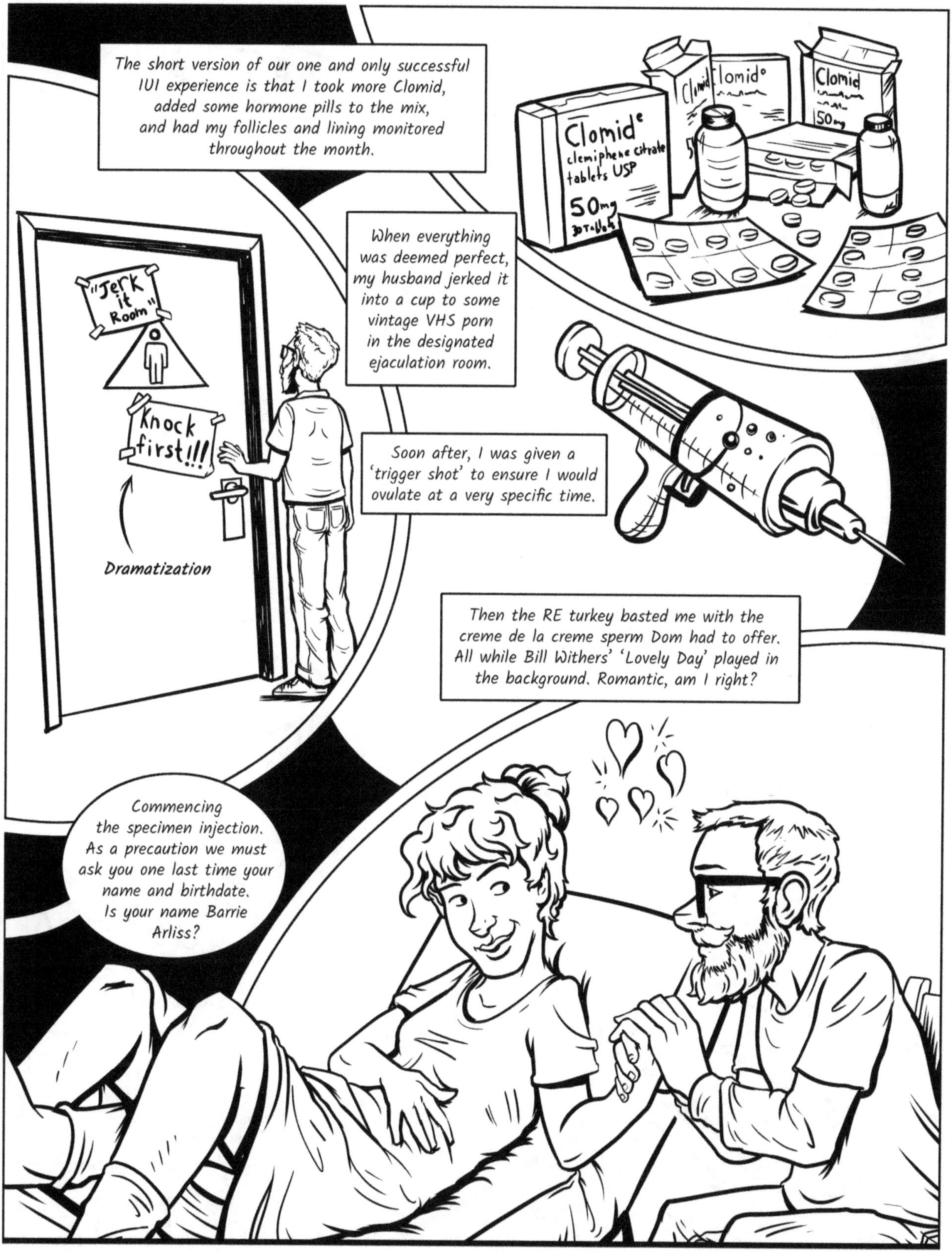
The short version of our one and only successful IUI experience is that I took more Clomid, added some hormone pills to the mix, and had my follicles and lining monitored throughout the month.
Clomid
clemiphene citrate tablets USP
50mg
Clomid
Clomid
50mg
When everything was deemed perfect, my husband jerked it into a cup to some vintage VHS porn in the designated ejaculation room.
"Jerk it Room"
Knock first!!!
Dramatization
Soon after, I was given a 'trigger shot' to ensure I would ovulate at a very specific time.
Then the RE turkey basted me with the creme de la creme sperm Dom had to offer. All while Bill Withers' 'Lovely Day' played in the background. Romantic, am I right?
Commencing the specimen injection. As a precaution we must ask you one last time your name and birthdate. Is your name Barrie Arliss?

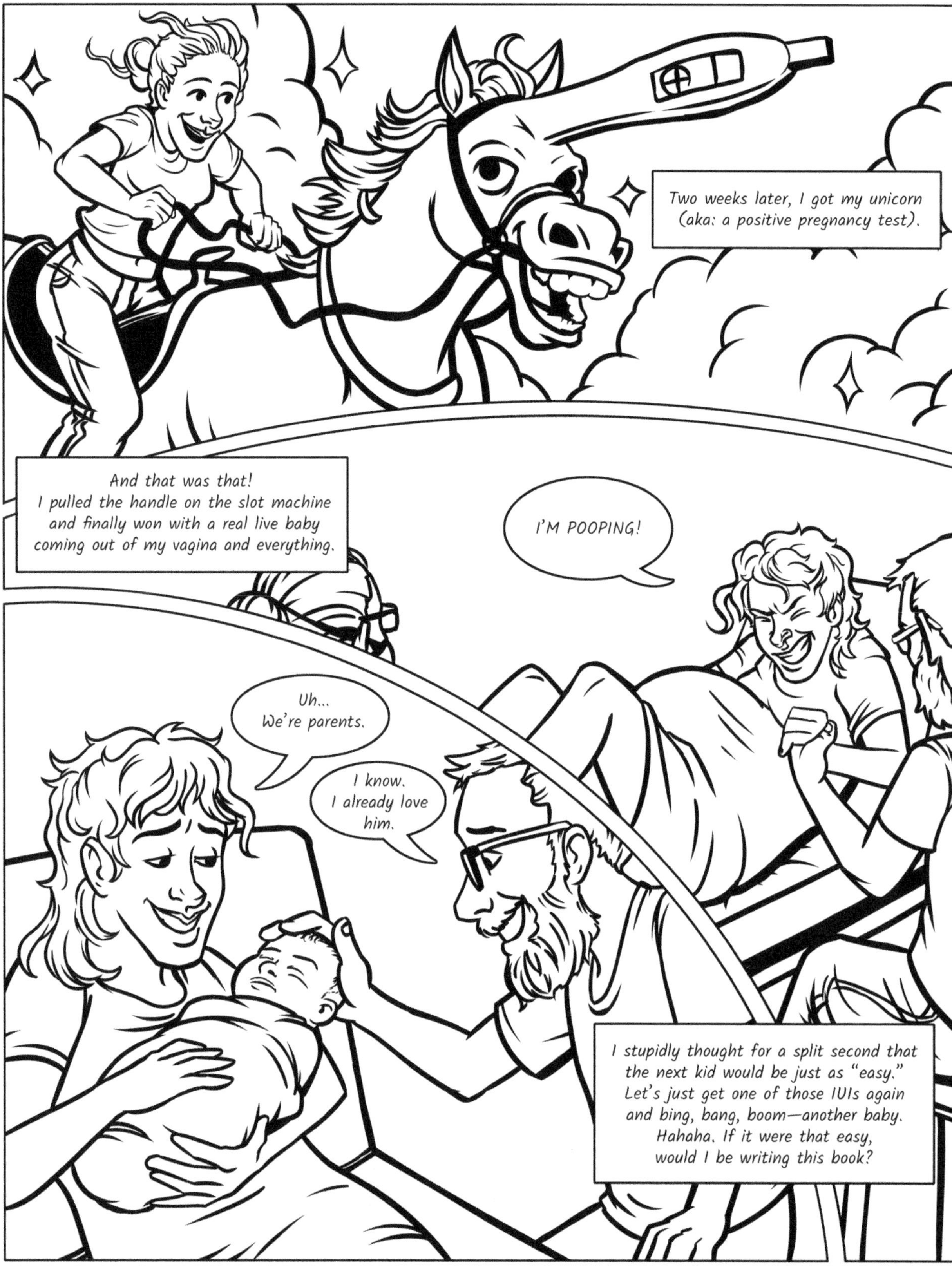
Two weeks later, I got my unicorn (aka: a positive pregnancy test).
And that was that! I pulled the handle on the slot machine and finally won with a real live baby coming out of my vagina and everything.
I'M POOPING!
Uh... We're parents.
I know. I already love him.
I stupidly thought for a split second that the next kid would be just as "easy." Let's just get one of those IUIs again and bing, bang, boom—another baby. Hahaha. If it were that easy, would I be writing this book?

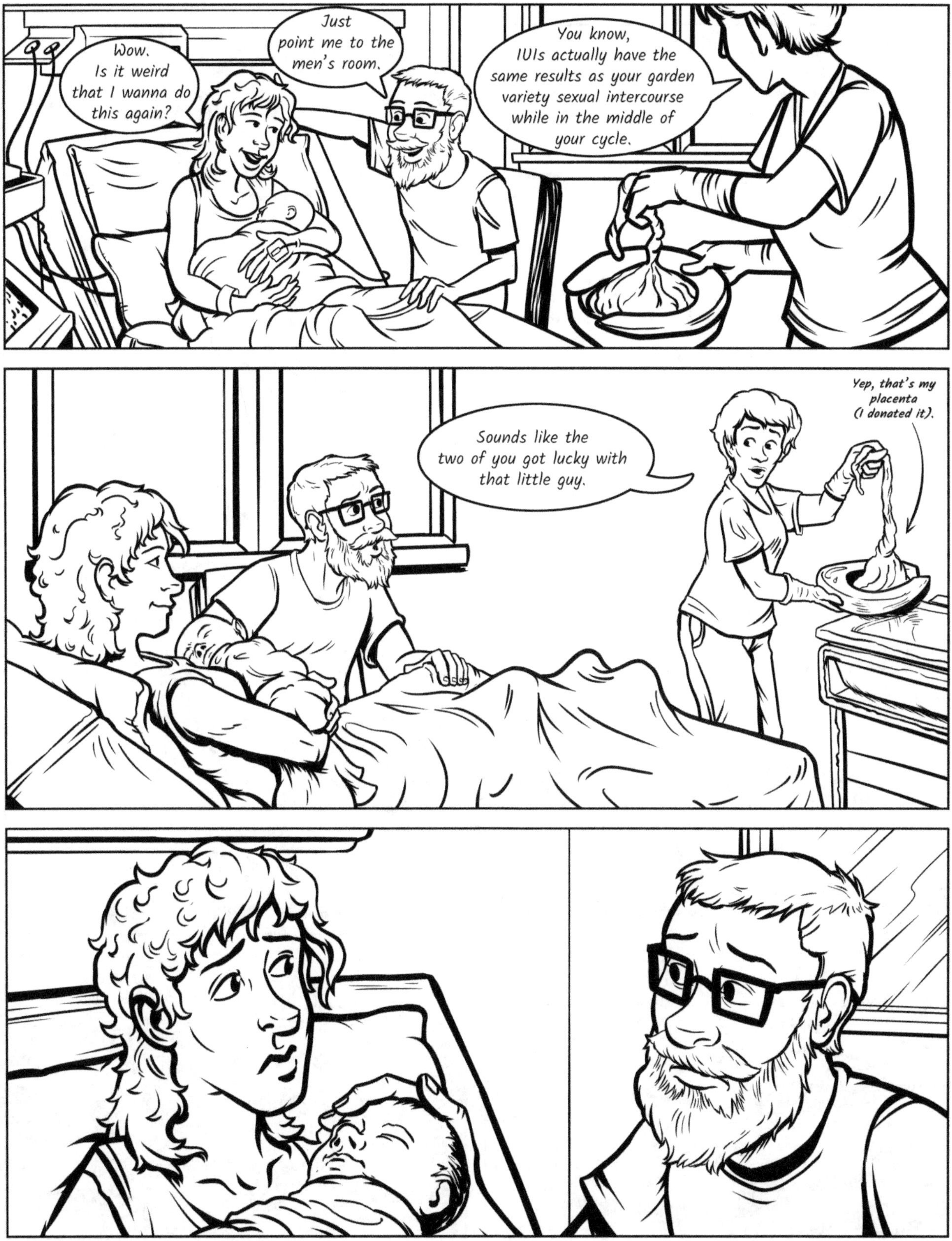
Wow. Is it weird that I wanna do this again?
Just point me to the men's room.
You know, IUIs actually have the same results as your garden variety sexual intercourse while in the middle of your cycle.
Sounds like the two of you got lucky with that little guy.
Yep, that's my placenta (I donated it).

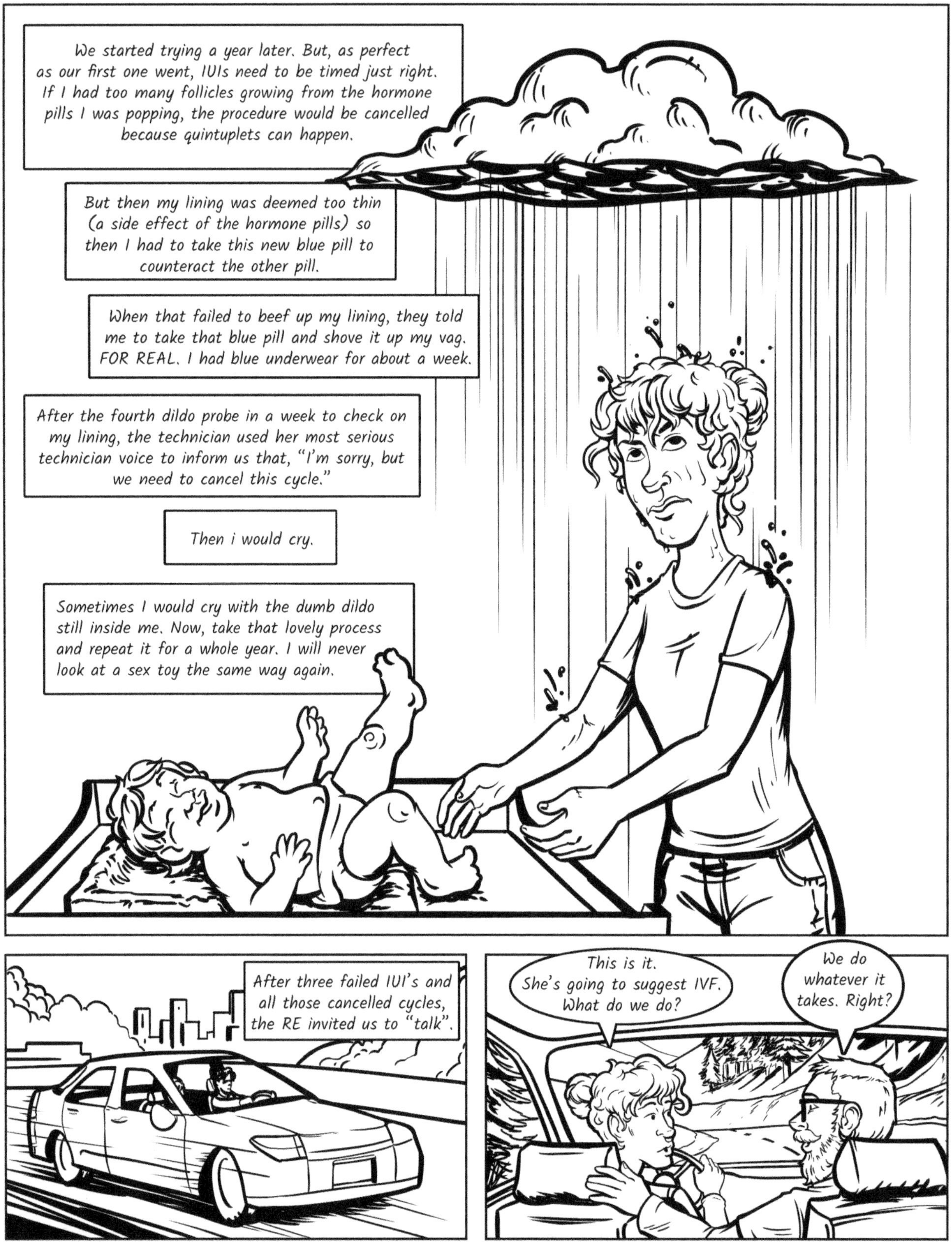
We started trying a year later. But, as perfect as our first one went, IUIs need to be timed just right. If I had too many follicles growing from the hormone pills I was popping, the procedure would be cancelled because quintuplets can happen.
But then my lining was deemed too thin (a side effect of the hormone pills) so then I had to take this new blue pill to counteract the other pill.
When that failed to beef up my lining, they told me to take that blue pill and shove it up my vag. FOR REAL. I had blue underwear for about a week.
After the fourth dildo probe in a week to check on my lining, the technician used her most serious technician voice to inform us that, "I'm sorry, but we need to cancel this cycle."
Then i would cry.
Sometimes I would cry with the dumb dildo still inside me. Now, take that lovely process and repeat it for a whole year. I will never look at a sex toy the same way again.
After three failed IUI's and all those cancelled cycles, the RE invited us to "talk".
This is it. She's going to suggest IVF. What do we do?
We do whatever it takes. Right?

Do's And So Many Don'ts

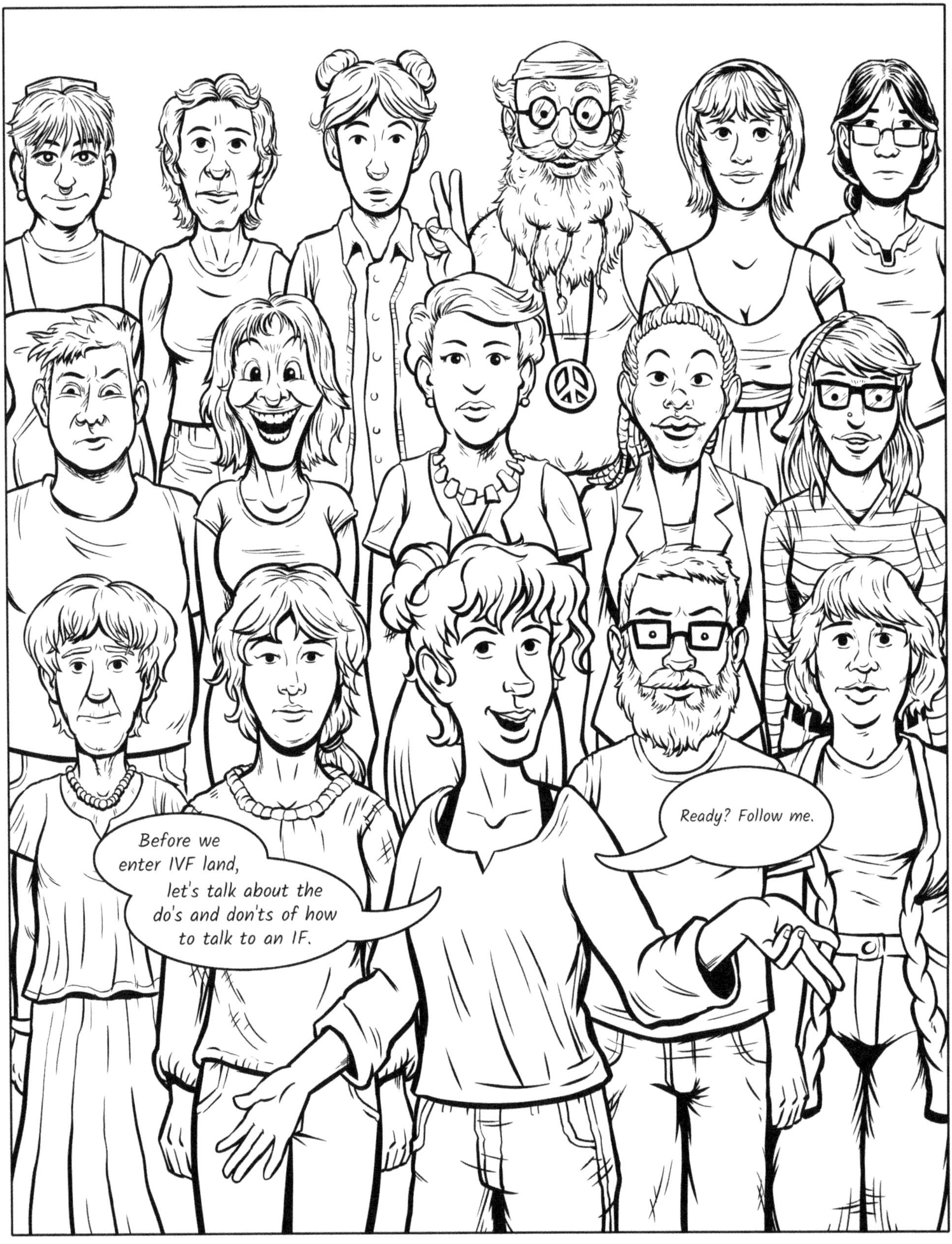
Before we enter IVF land, let's talk about the do's and don'ts of how to talk to an IF.
Ready? Follow me.

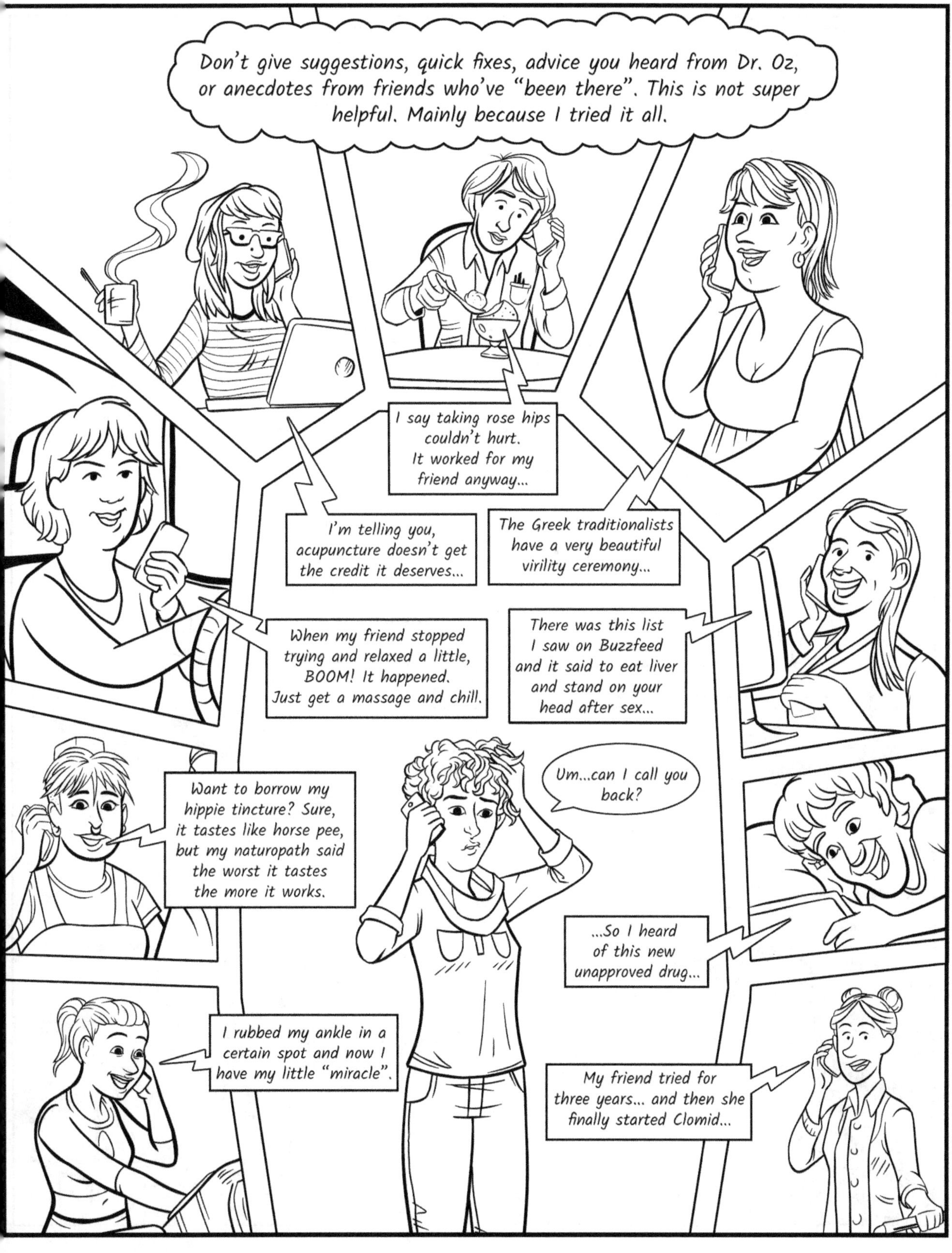
Don't give suggestions, quick fixes, advice you heard from Dr. Oz, or anecdotes from friends who've "been there". This is not super helpful. Mainly because I tried it all.
I say taking rose hips couldn't hurt. It worked for my friend anyway...
I'm telling you, acupuncture doesn't get the credit it deserves...
The Greek traditionalists have a very beautiful virility ceremony...
When my friend stopped trying and relaxed a little, BOOM! It happened. Just get a massage and chill.
There was this list I saw on Buzzfeed and it said to eat liver and stand on your head after sex...
Want to borrow my hippie tincture? Sure, it tastes like horse pee, but my naturopath said the worst it tastes the more it works.
Um...can I call you back?
...So I heard of this new unapproved drug...
I rubbed my ankle in a certain spot and now I have my little "miracle".
My friend tried for three years... and then she finally started Clomid...

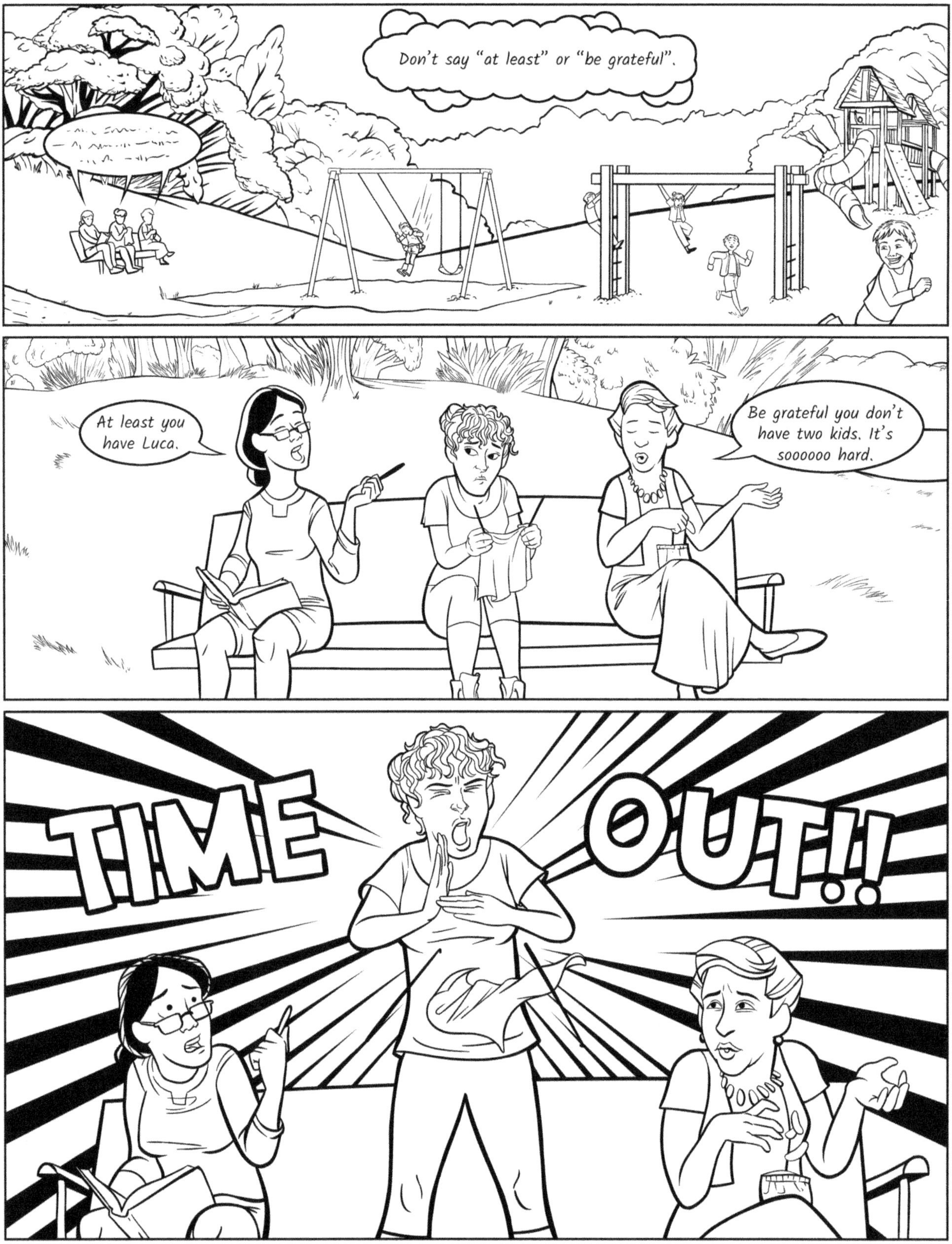
Don't say "at least" or "be grateful".
At least you have Luca.
Be grateful you don't have two kids. It's soooooo hard.
TIME OUT!!

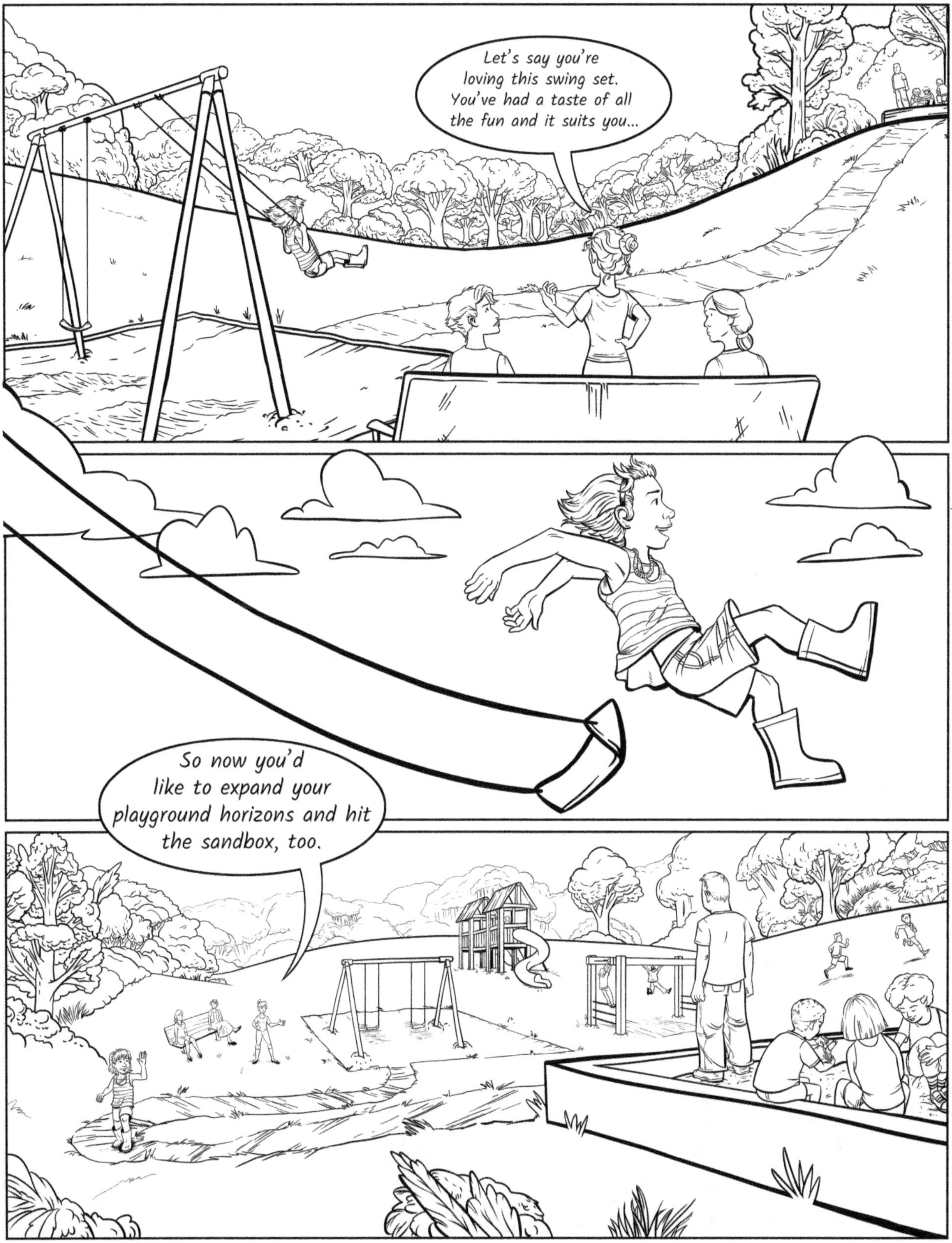
Let's say you're loving this swing set. You've had a taste of all the fun and it suits you...
So now you'd like to expand your playground horizons and hit the sandbox, too.

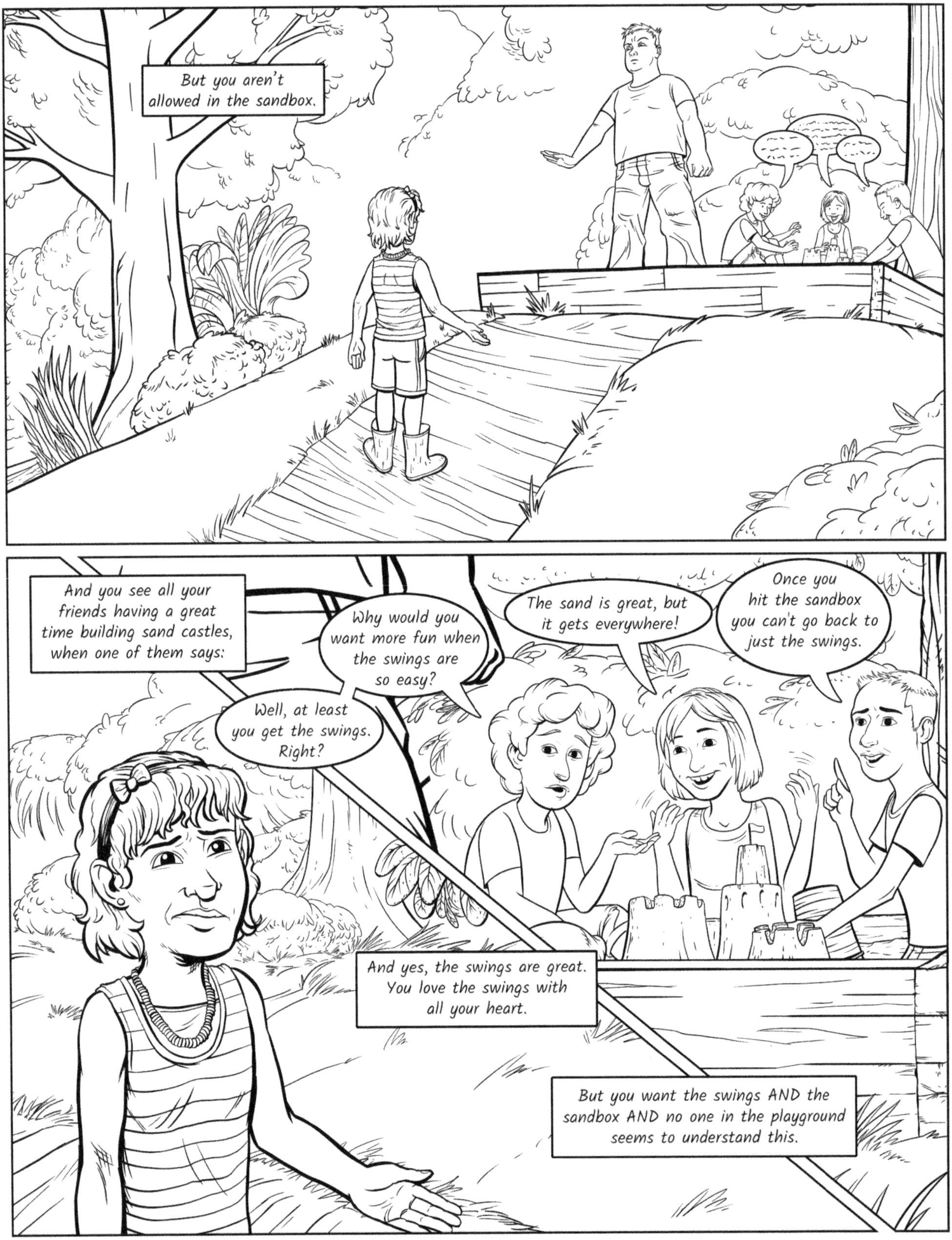
But you aren't allowed in the sandbox.
And you see all your friends having a great time building sand castles, when one of them says:
Why would you want more fun when the swings are so easy?
The sand is great, but it gets everywhere!
Once you hit the sandbox you can't go back to just the swings.
Well, at least you get the swings. Right?
And yes, the swings are great. You love the swings with all your heart.
But you want the swings AND the sandbox AND no one in the playground seems to understand this.

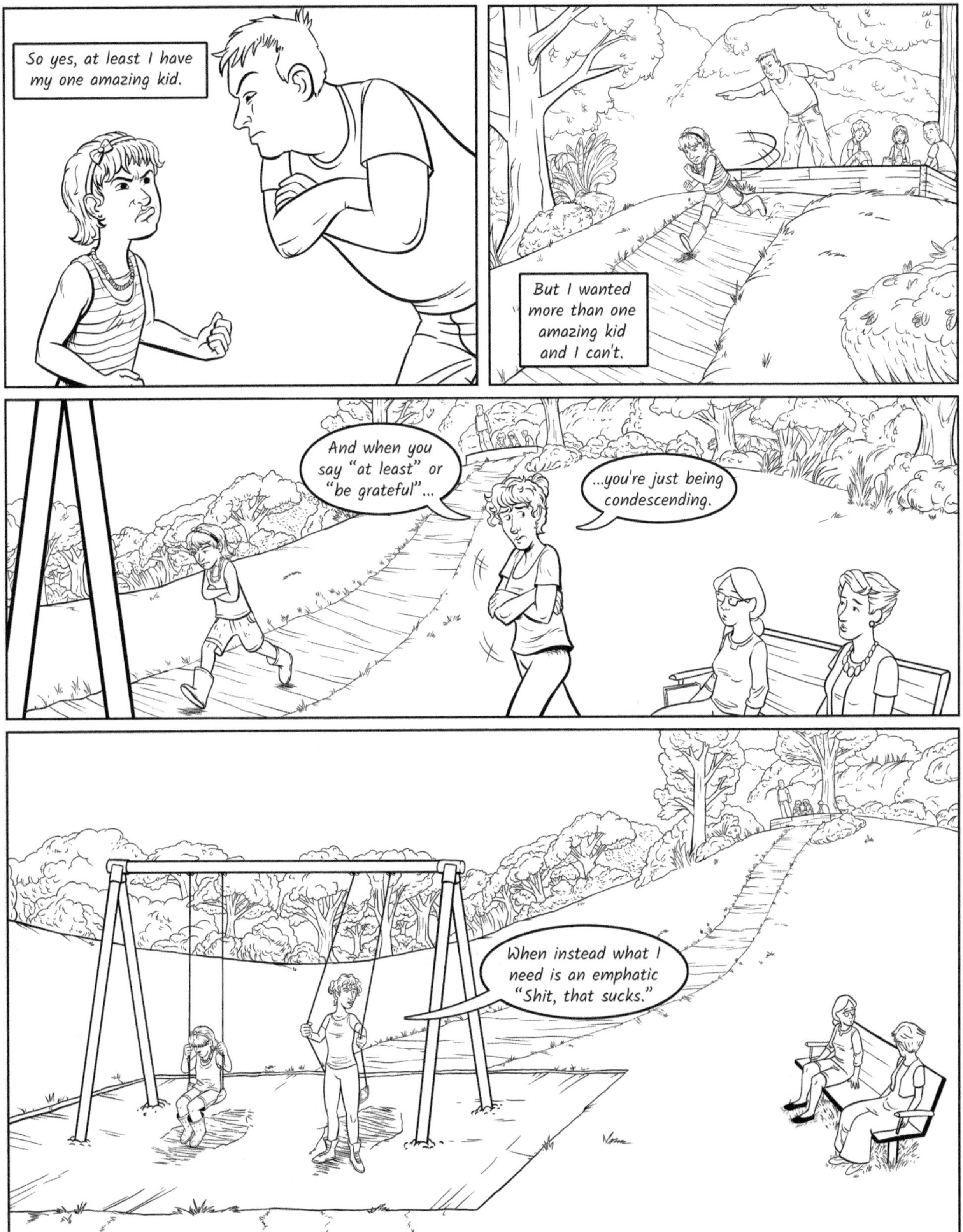
So yes, at least I have my one amazing kid.
But I wanted more than one amazing kid and I can't.
And when you say "at least" or "be grateful"...
...you're just being condescending.
When instead what I need is an emphatic "Shit, that sucks."

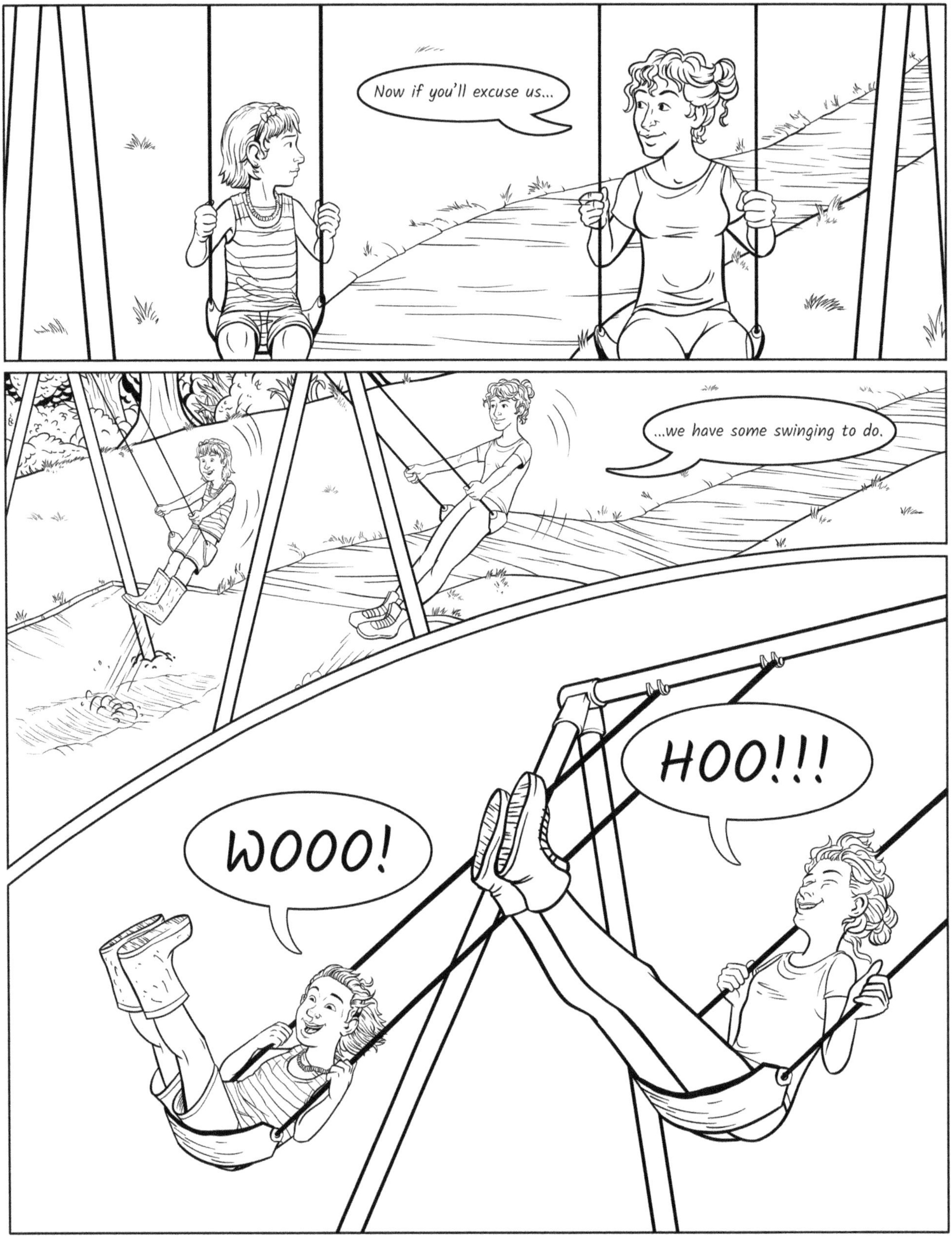
Now if you'll excuse us...
...we have some swinging to do.
WOOO!
HOO!!!

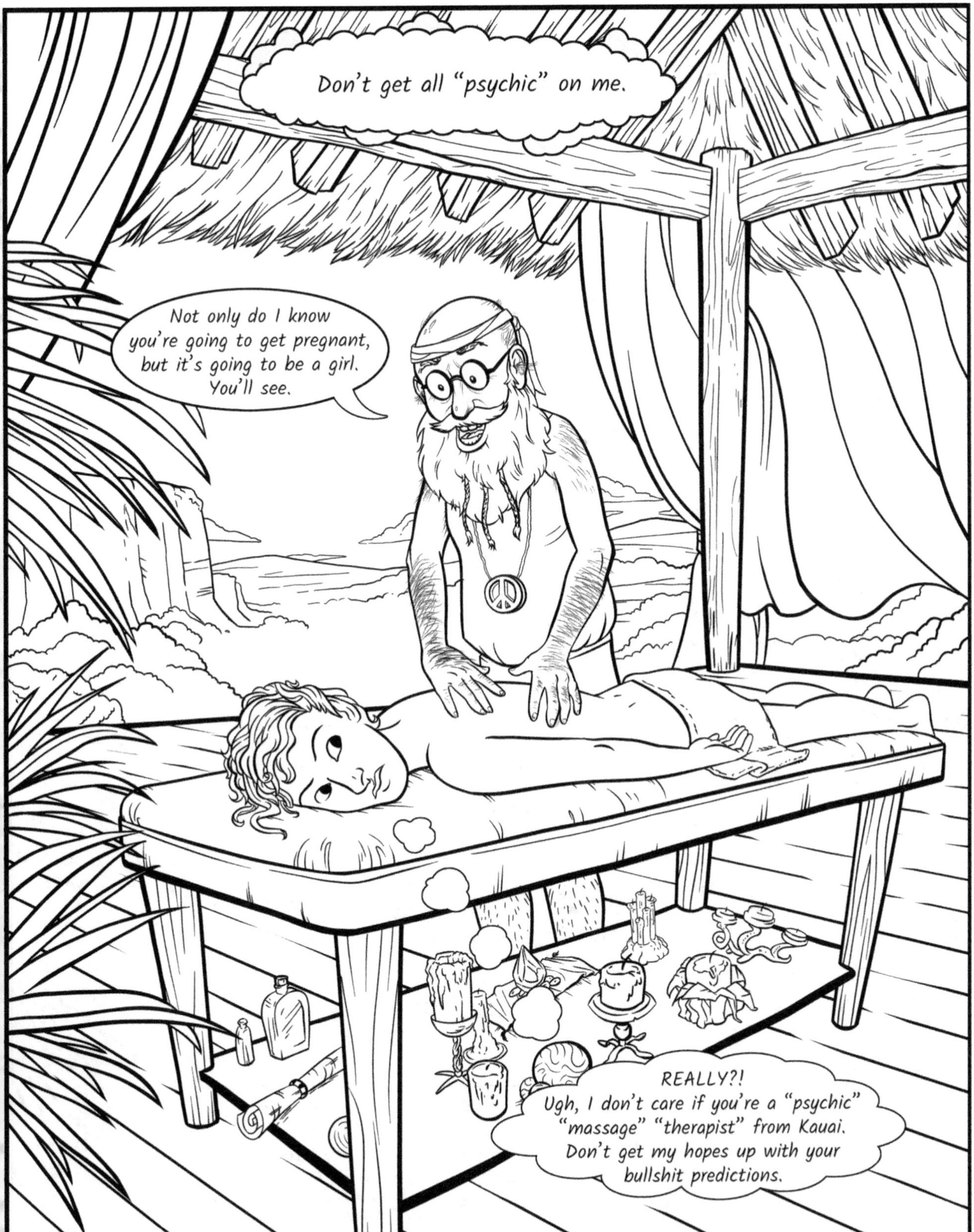
Don't get all "psychic" on me.
Not only do I know you're going to get pregnant, but it's going to be a girl. You'll see.
REALLY?! Ugh, I don't care if you're a "psychic" "massage" "therapist" from Kauai. Don't get my hopes up with your bullshit predictions.

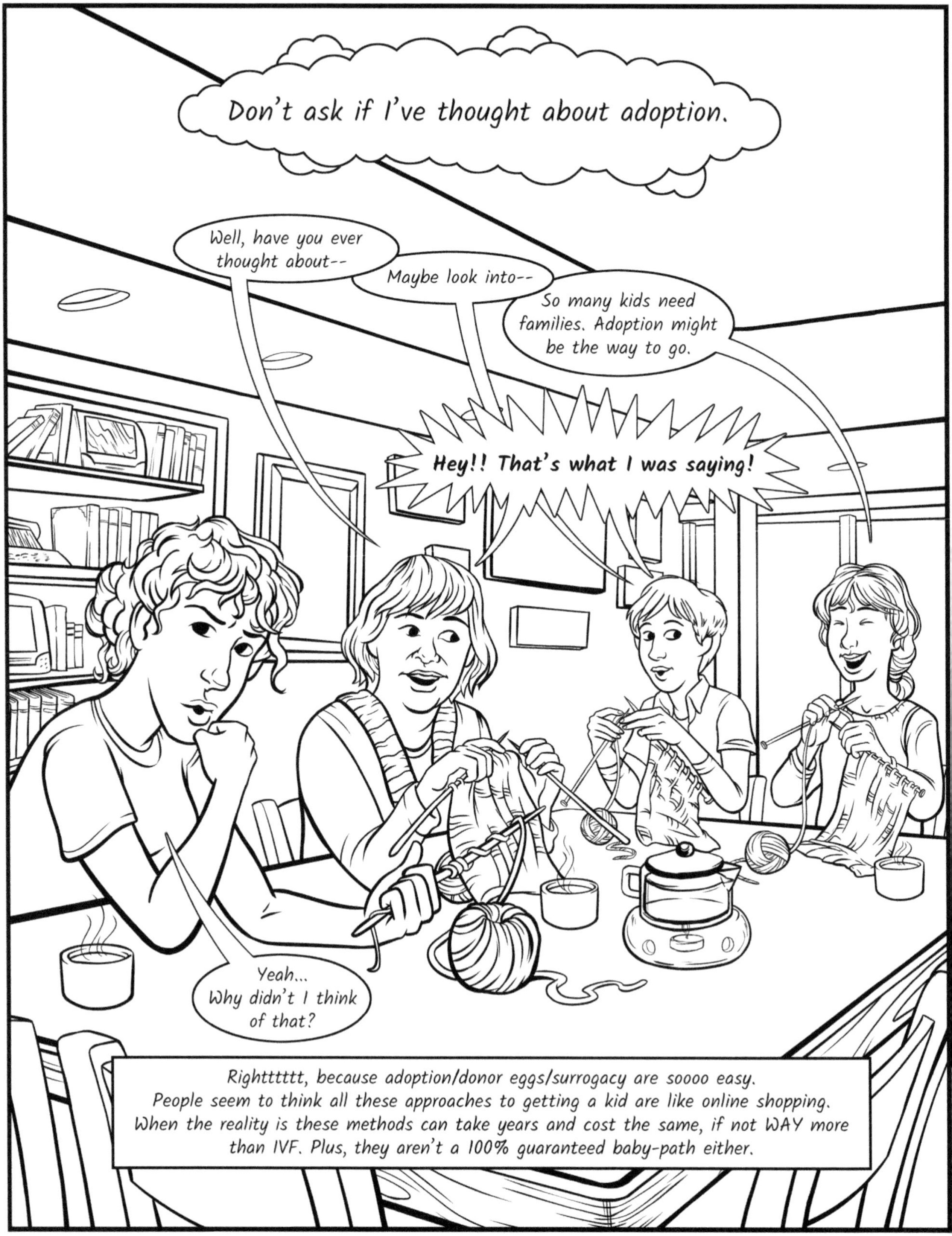
Don't ask if I've thought about adoption.
Well, have you ever thought about--
Maybe look into--
So many kids need families. Adoption might be the way to go.
Hey!! That's what I was saying!
Yeah... Why didn't I think of that?
Righttttttt, because adoption/donor eggs/surrogacy are soooo easy. People seem to think all these approaches to getting a kid are like online shopping. When the reality is these methods can take years and cost the same, if not WAY more than IVF. Plus, they aren't a 100% guaranteed baby-path either.

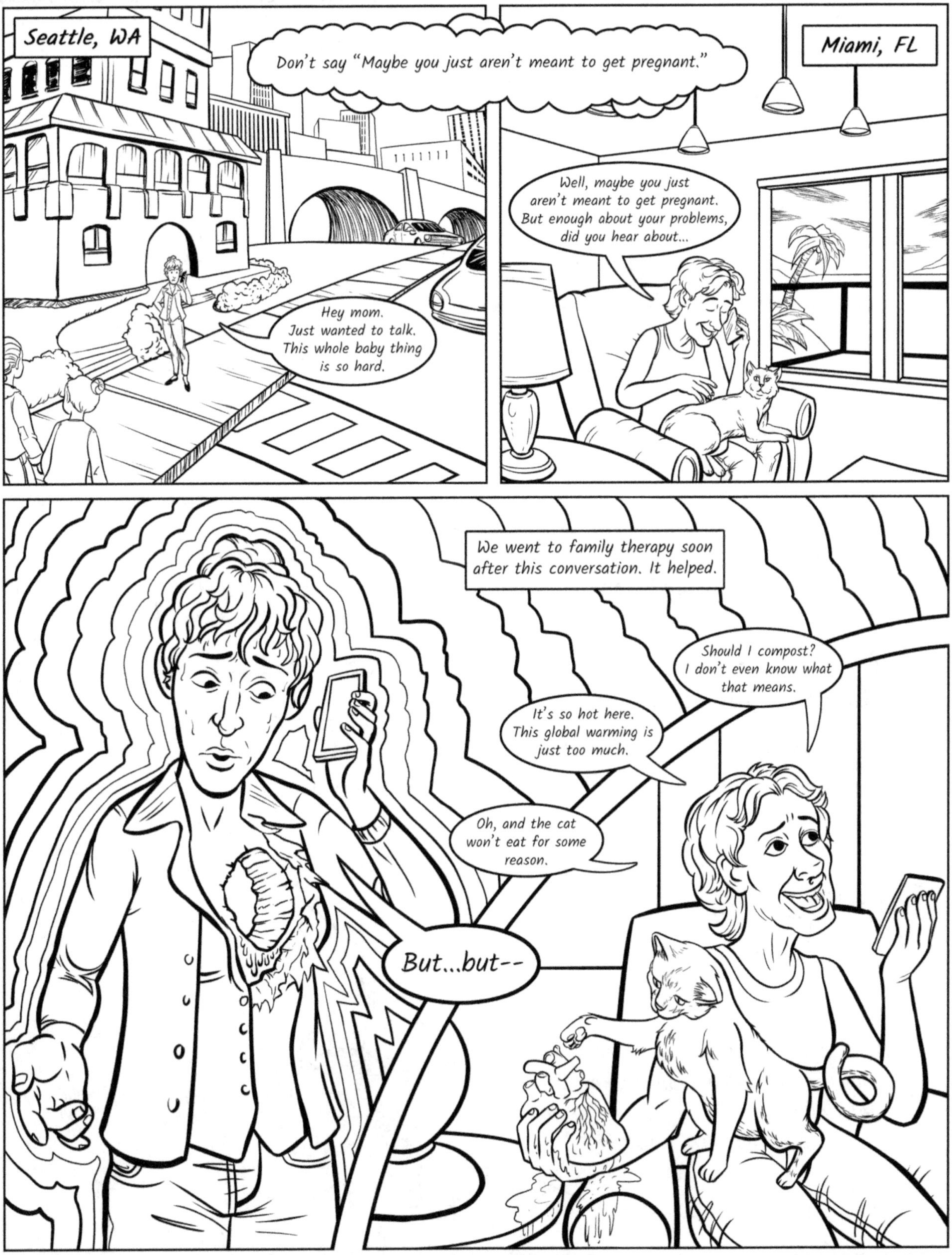
Seattle, WA
Don't say "Maybe you just aren't meant to get pregnant."
Miami, FL
Hey mom. Just wanted to talk. This whole baby thing is so hard.
Well, maybe you just aren't meant to get pregnant. But enough about your problems, did you hear about...
We went to family therapy soon after this conversation. It helped.
Should I compost? I don't even know what that means.
It's so hot here. This global warming is just too much.
Oh, and the cat won't eat for some reason.
But...but--

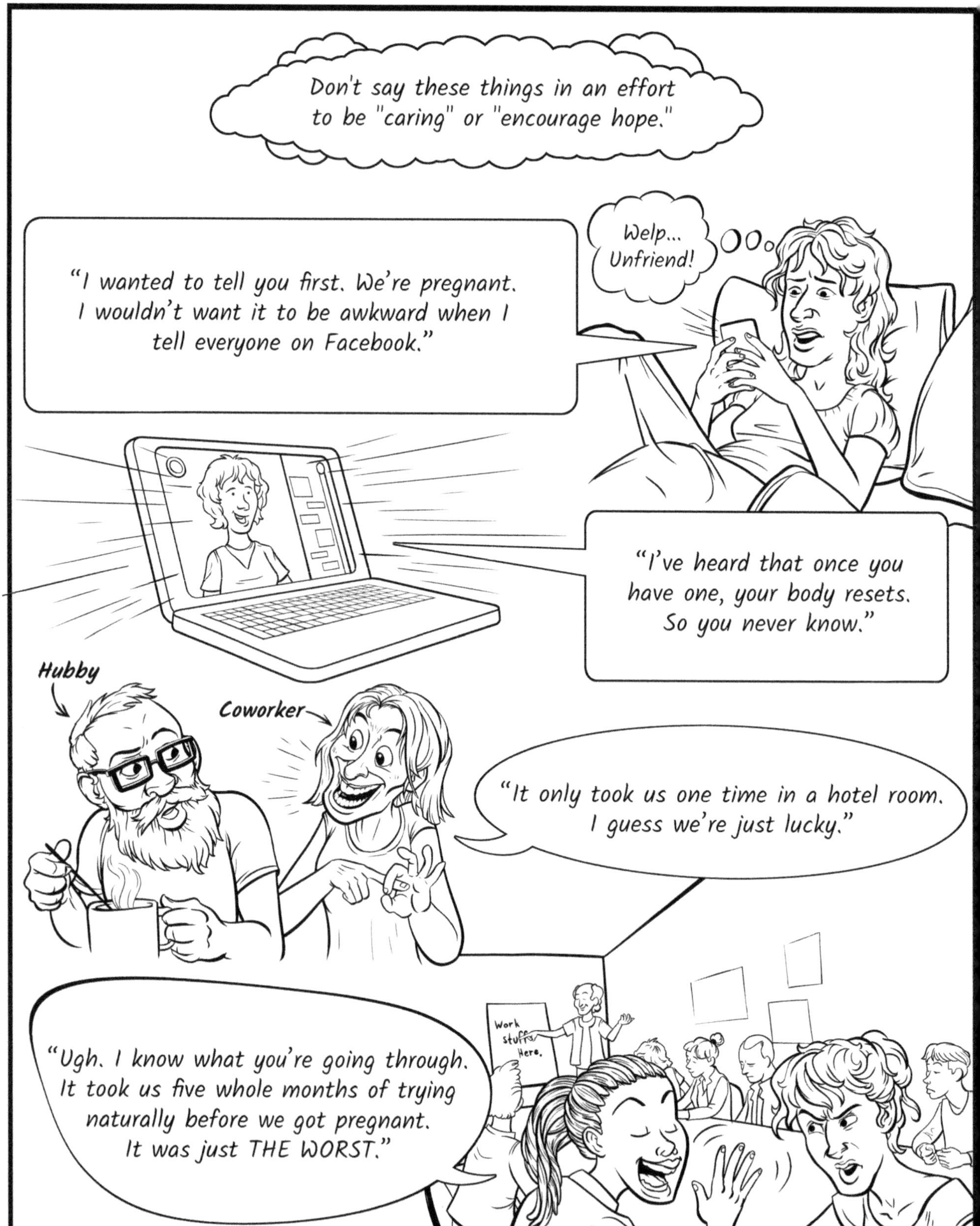
Don't say these things in an effort to be "caring" or "encourage hope."
"I wanted to tell you first. We're pregnant. I wouldn't want it to be awkward when I tell everyone on Facebook."
Welp... Unfriend!
"I've heard that once you have one, your body resets. So you never know."
Hubby
Coworker
"It only took us one time in a hotel room. I guess we're just lucky."
"Ugh. I know what you're going through. It took us five whole months of trying naturally before we got pregnant. It was just THE WORST."
Work stuff Here.

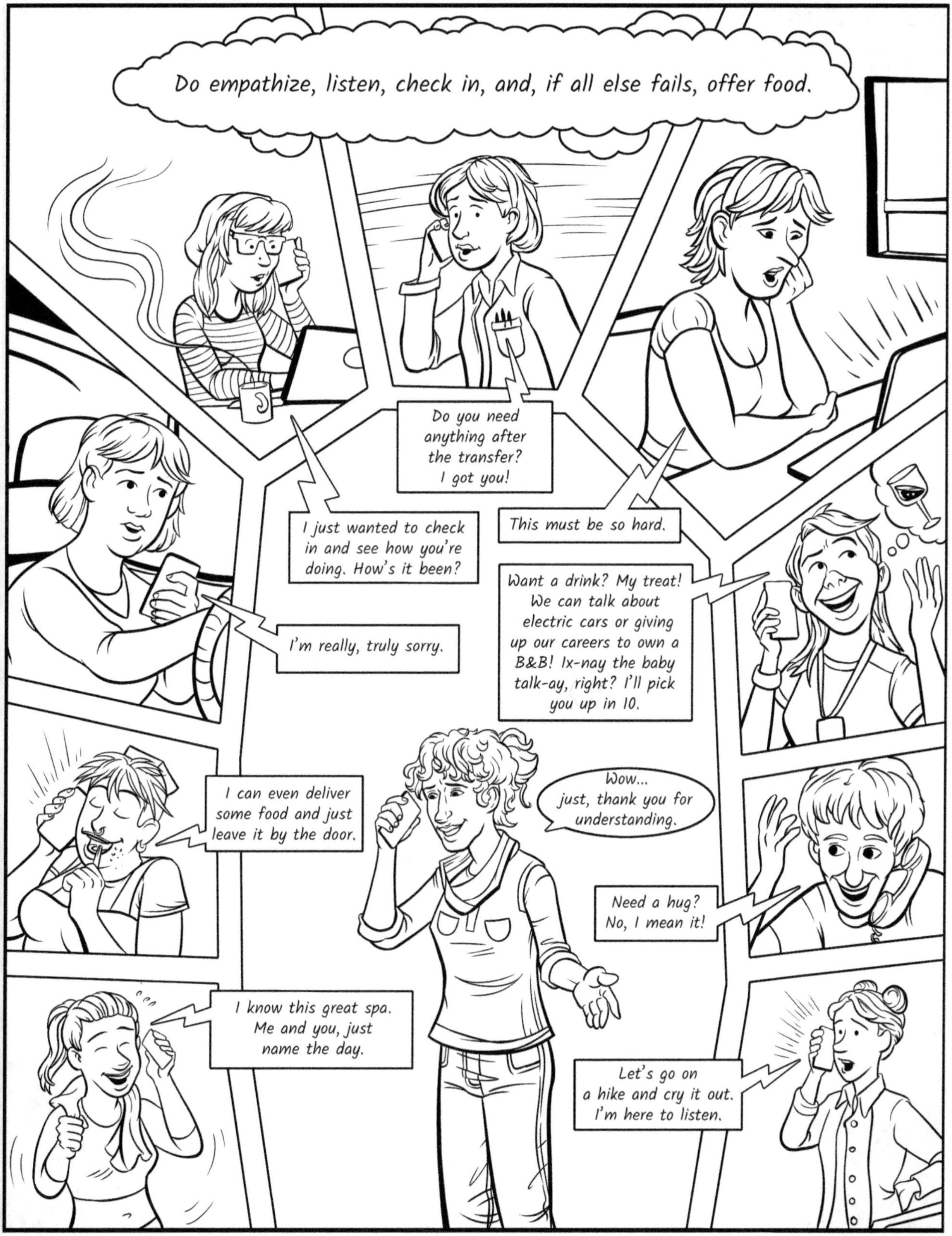

Do empathize, listen, check in, and, if all else fails, offer food.
Do you need anything after the transfer? I got you!
I just wanted to check in and see how you're doing. How's it been?
This must be so hard.
I'm really, truly sorry.
Want a drink? My treat! We can talk about electric cars or giving up our careers to own a B&B! Ix-nay the baby talk-ay, right? I'll pick you up in 10.
I can even deliver some food and just leave it by the door.
Wow... just, thank you for understanding.
Need a hug? No, I mean it!
I know this great spa. Me and you, just name the day.
Let's go on a hike and cry it out. I'm here to listen.

The First Time I Shot Myself

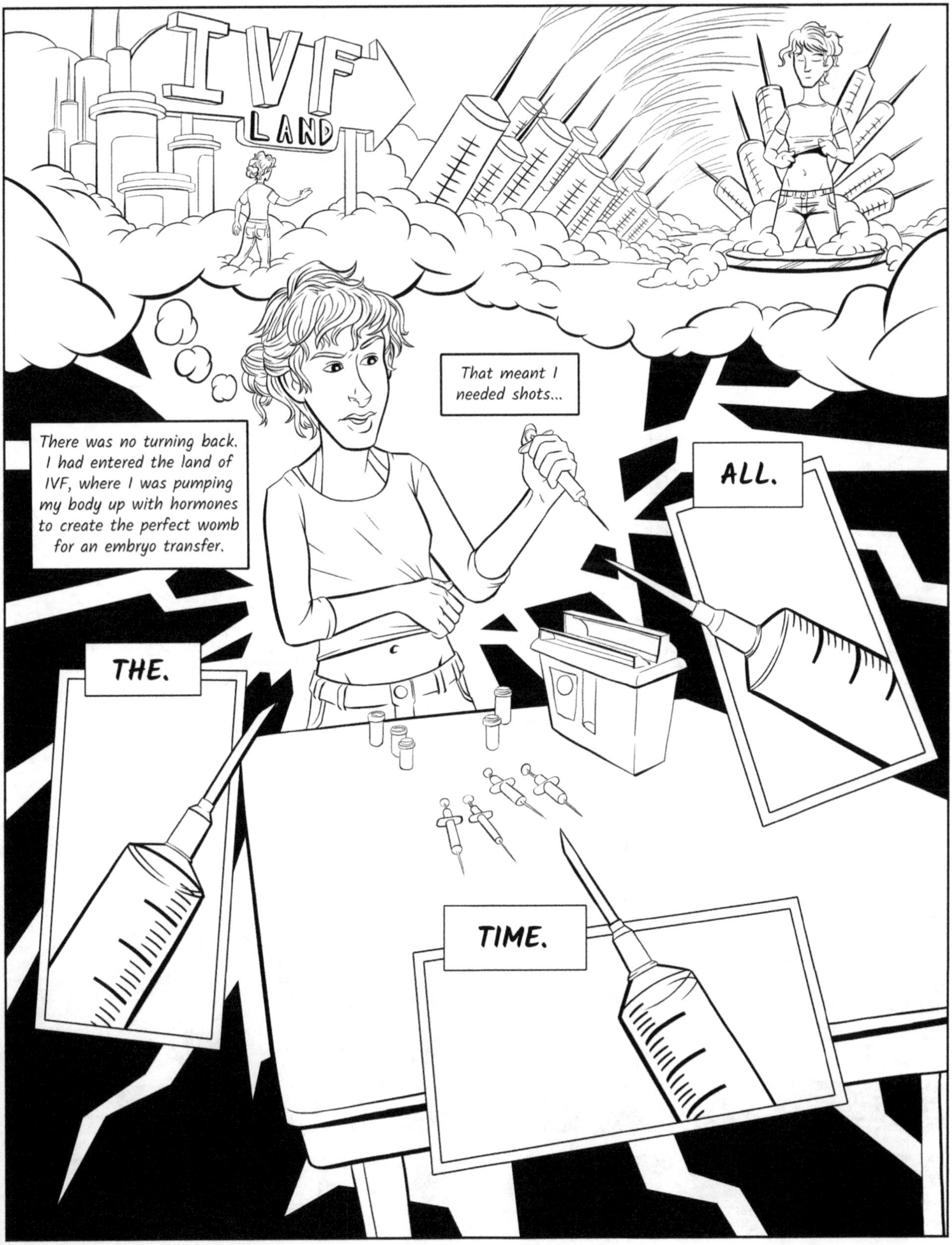
IVF
LAND
That meant I needed shots...
There was no turning back. I had entered the land of IVF, where I was pumping my body up with hormones to create the perfect womb for an embryo transfer.
ALL.
THE.
TIME.

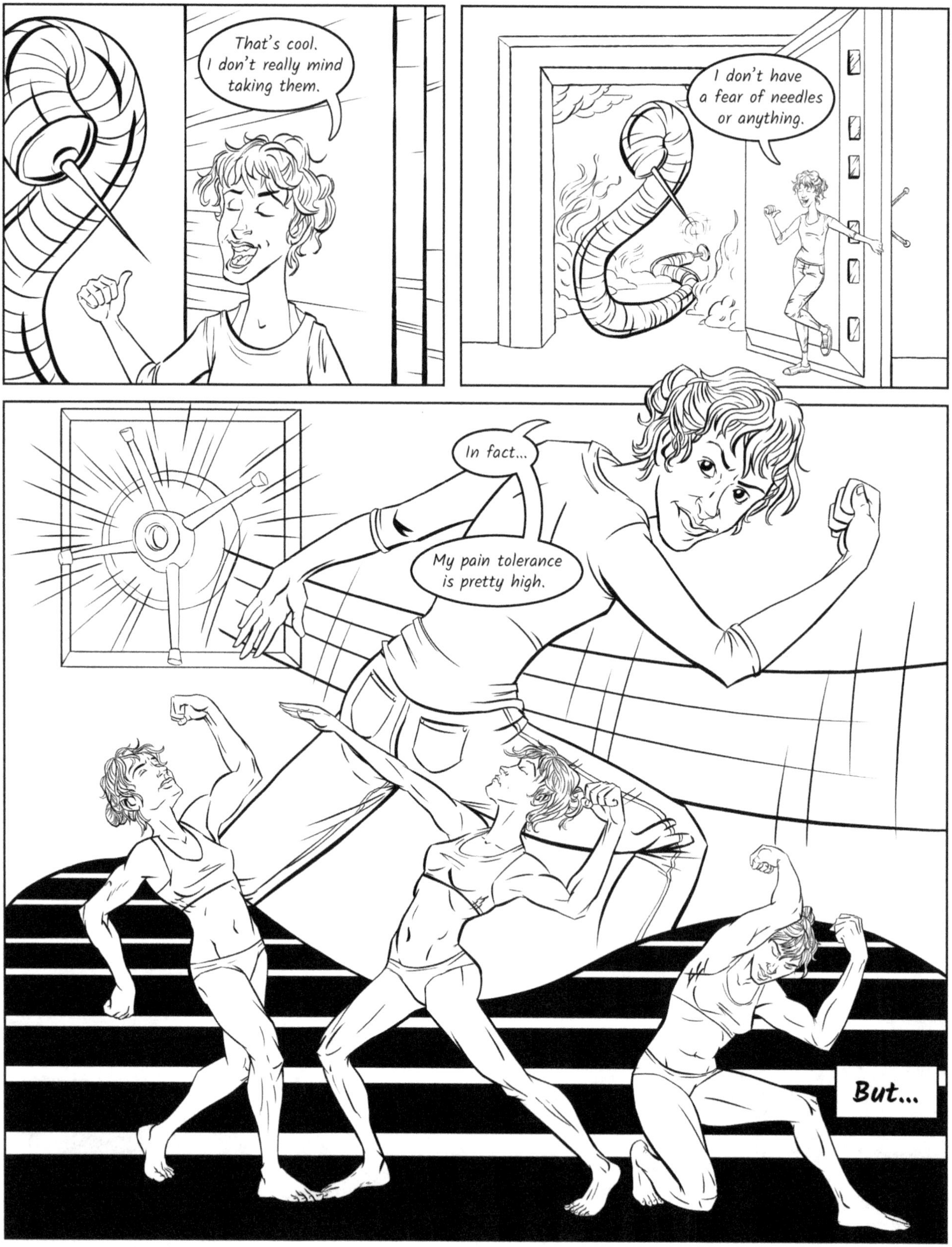
That's cool.
I don't really mind taking them.
I don't have a fear of needles or anything.
In fact...
My pain tolerance is pretty high.
But...

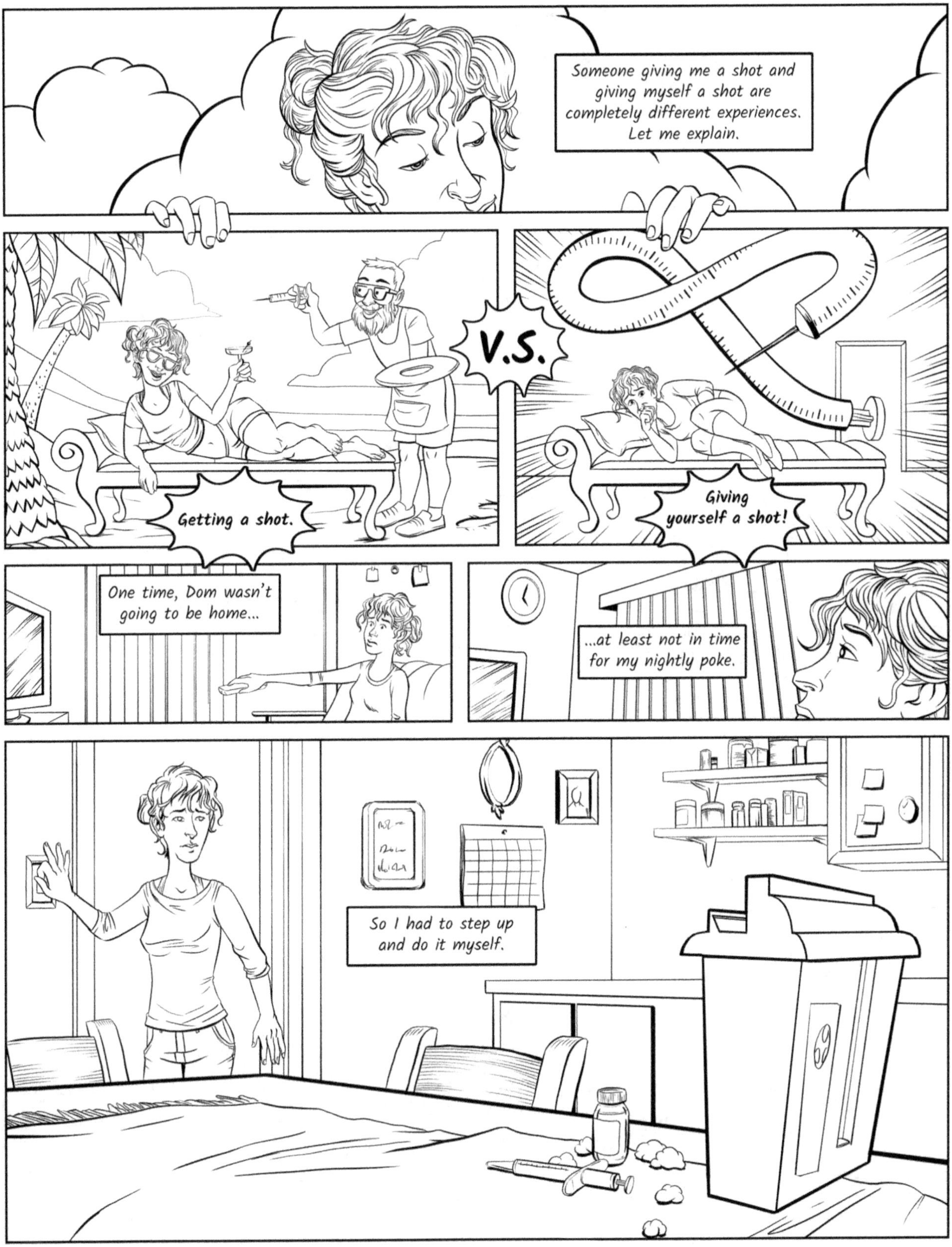
Someone giving me a shot and giving myself a shot are completely different experiences. Let me explain.
V.S.
Getting a shot.
Giving yourself a shot!
One time, Dom wasn't going to be home...
...at least not in time for my nightly poke.
So I had to step up and do it myself.

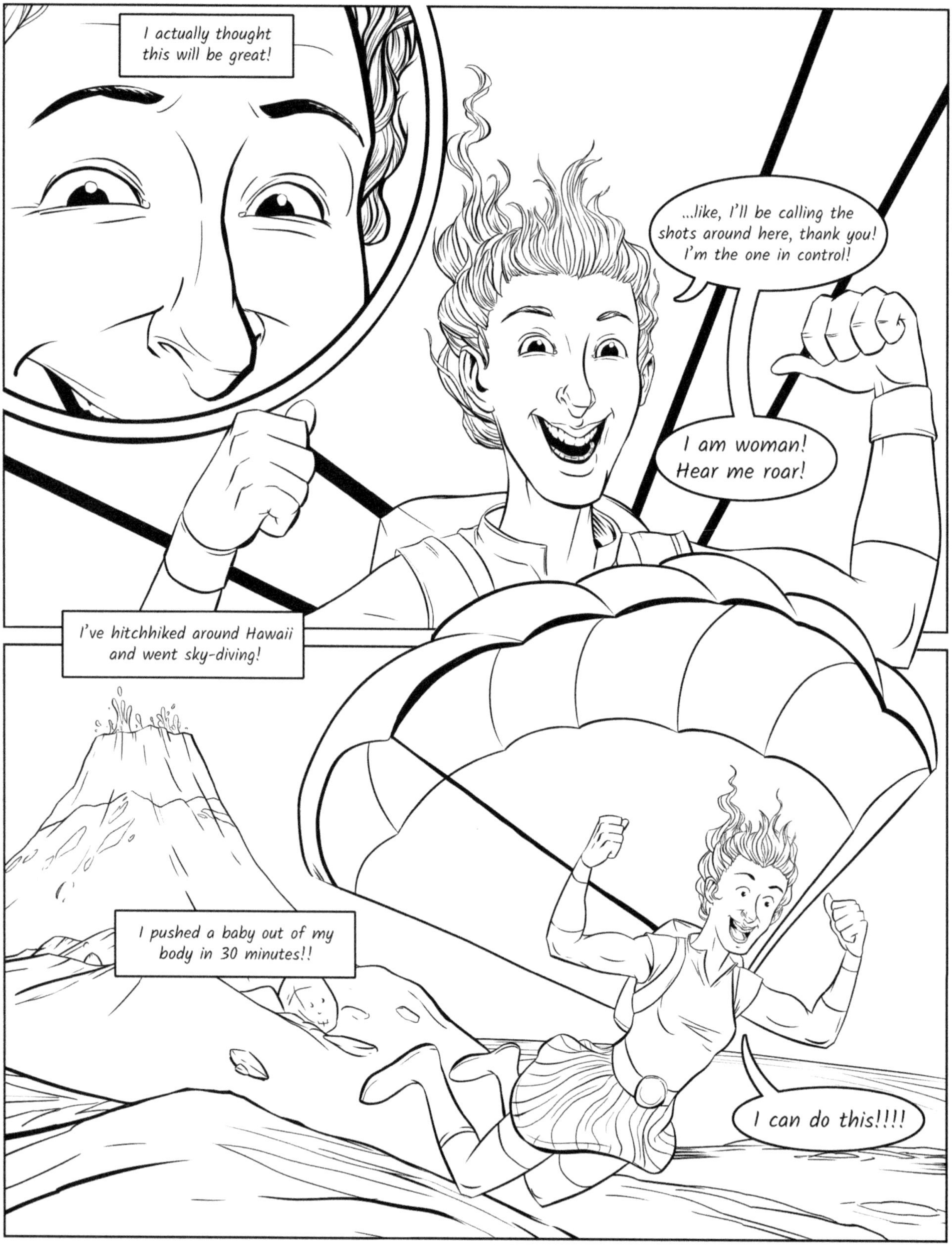
I actually thought this will be great!
...like, I'll be calling the shots around here, thank you! I'm the one in control!
I am woman! Hear me roar!
I've hitchhiked around Hawaii and went sky-diving!
I pushed a baby out of my body in 30 minutes!!
I can do this!!!!

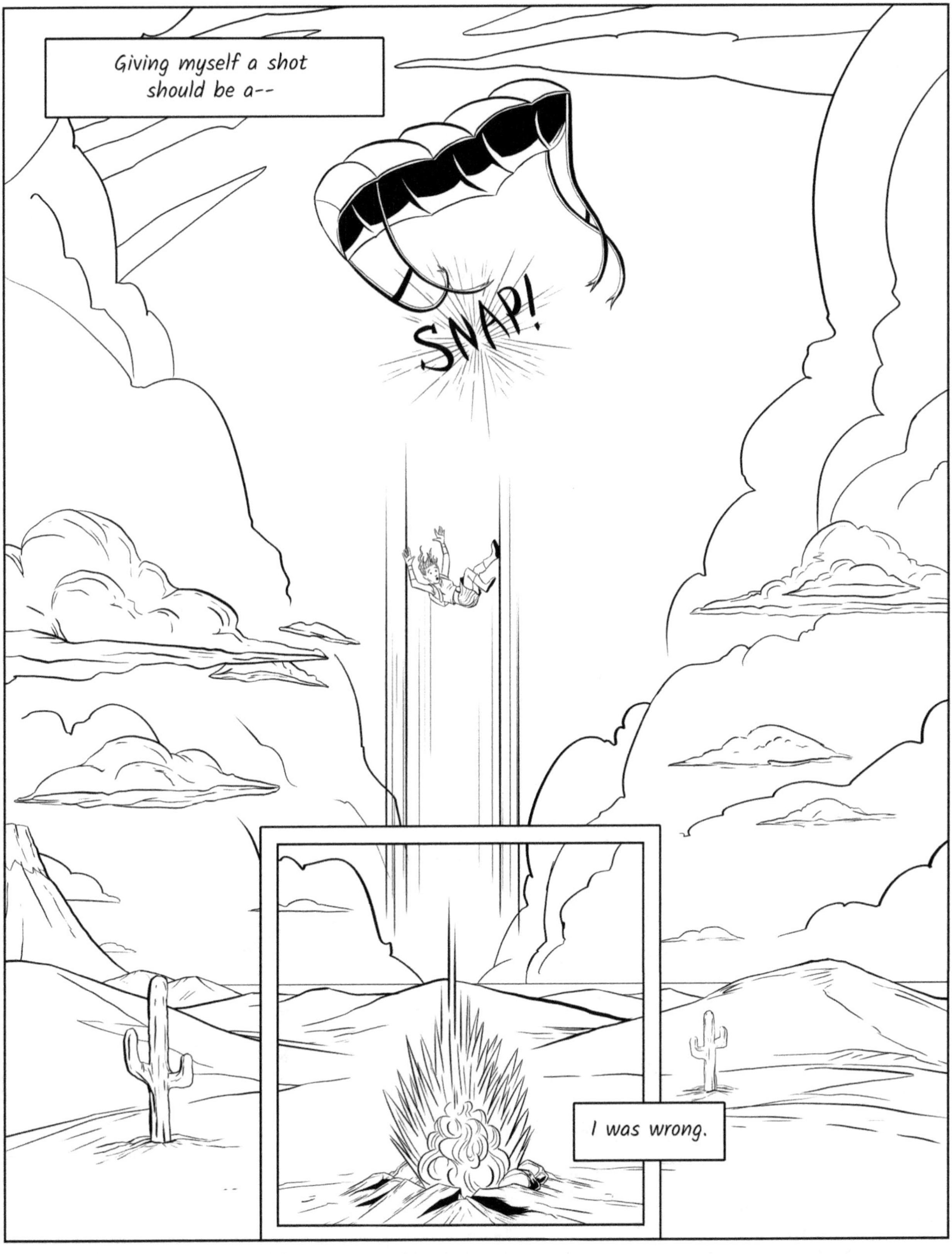
Giving myself a shot should be a--
SNAP!
I was wrong.

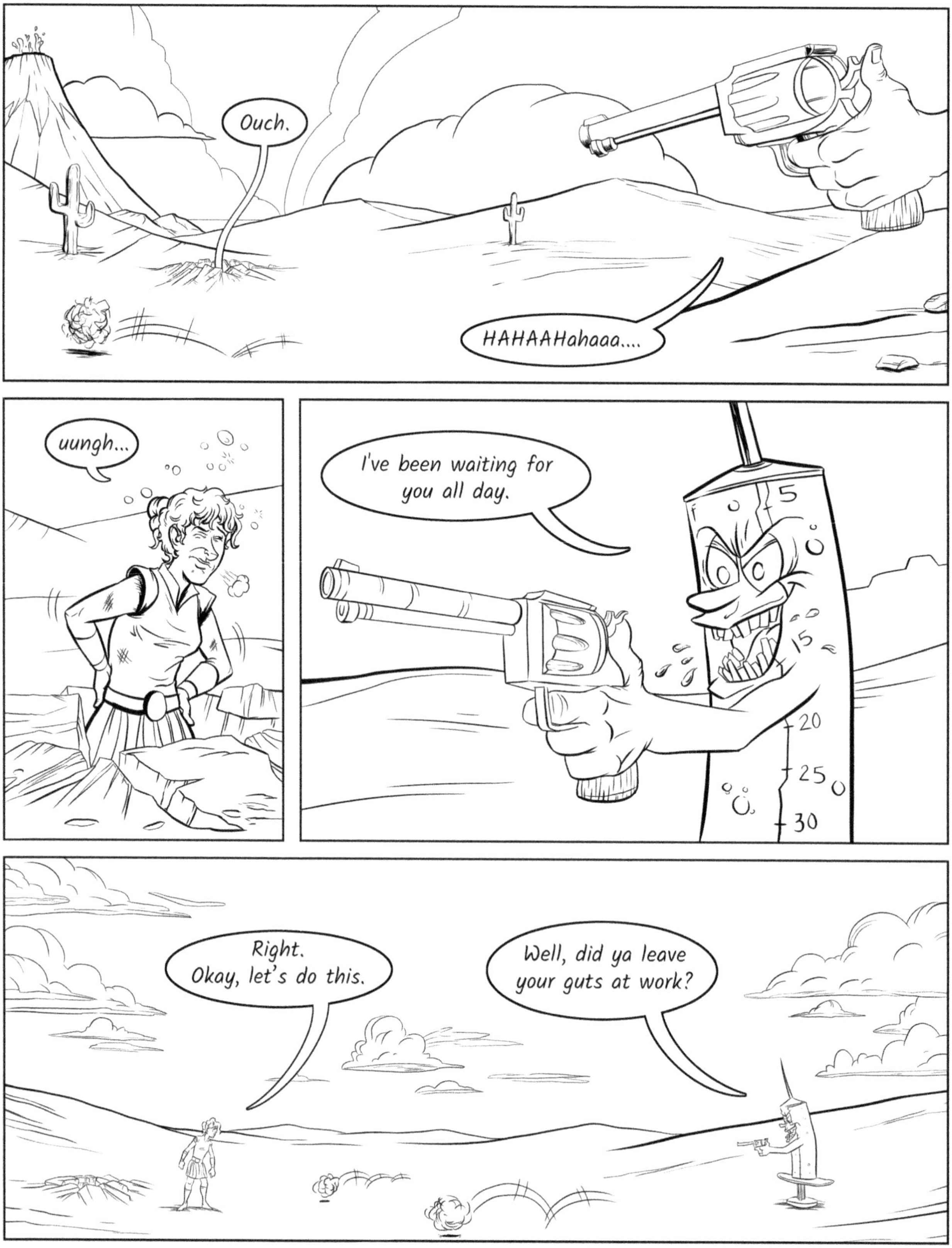
Ouch.
HAHAAHahaaa....
uungh...
I've been waiting for you all day.
5
15
20
25
30
Right. Okay, let's do this.
Well, did ya leave your guts at work?

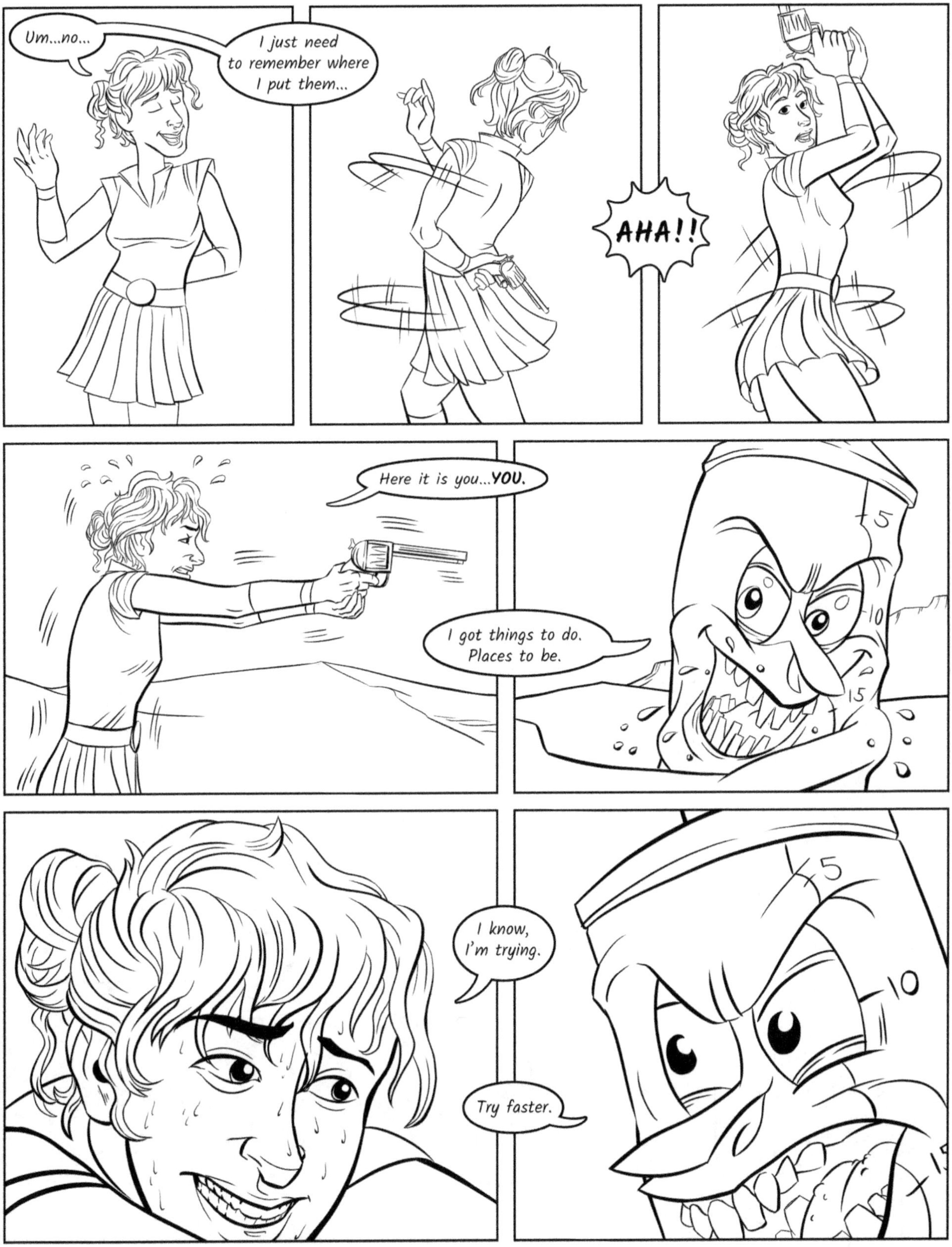
Um...no...
I just need to remember where I put them...
AHA!!
Here it is you...**YOU.**
I got things to do. Places to be.
5
10
15
I know, I'm trying.
Try faster.
5
10
15

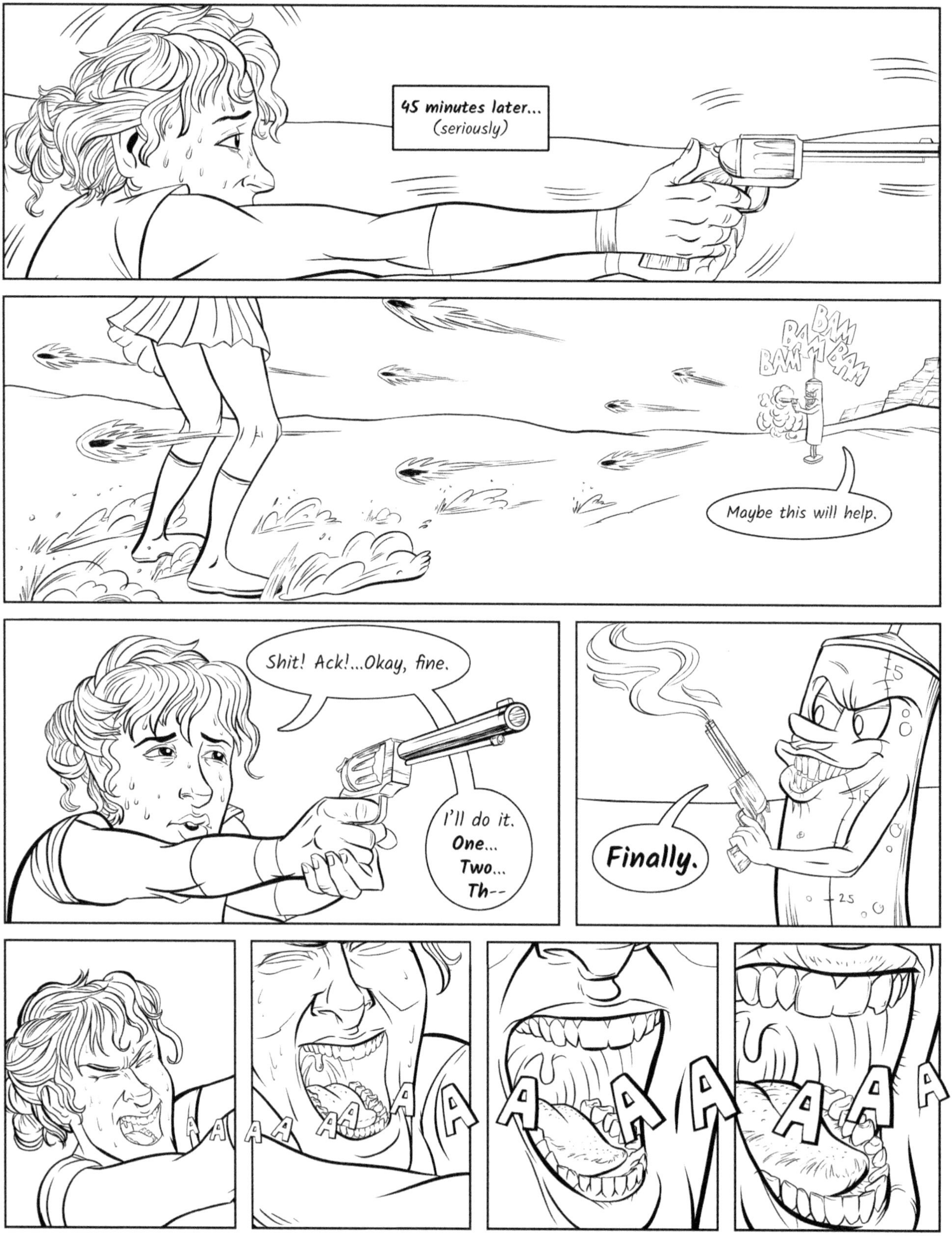
45 minutes later...
(seriously)
BAM BAM BAM BAM BAM
Maybe this will help.
Shit! Ack!...Okay, fine.
I'll do it. One... Two... Th--
Finally.
A A A A A A A A A A A A A A

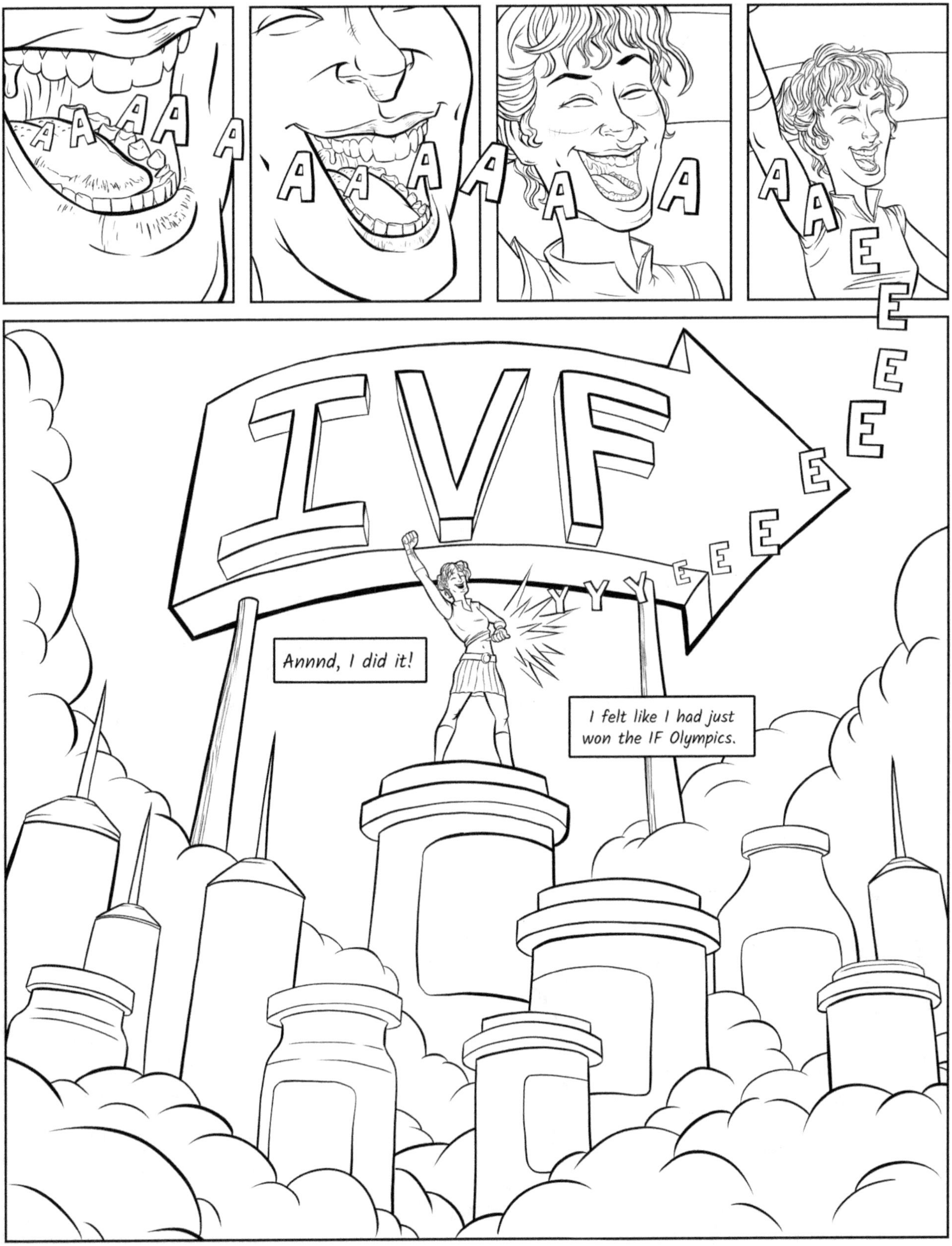
AAAAAAAAAAAAA
EEEEEEEEE
YYY
IVF
Annnd, I did it!
I felt like I had just won the IF Olympics.

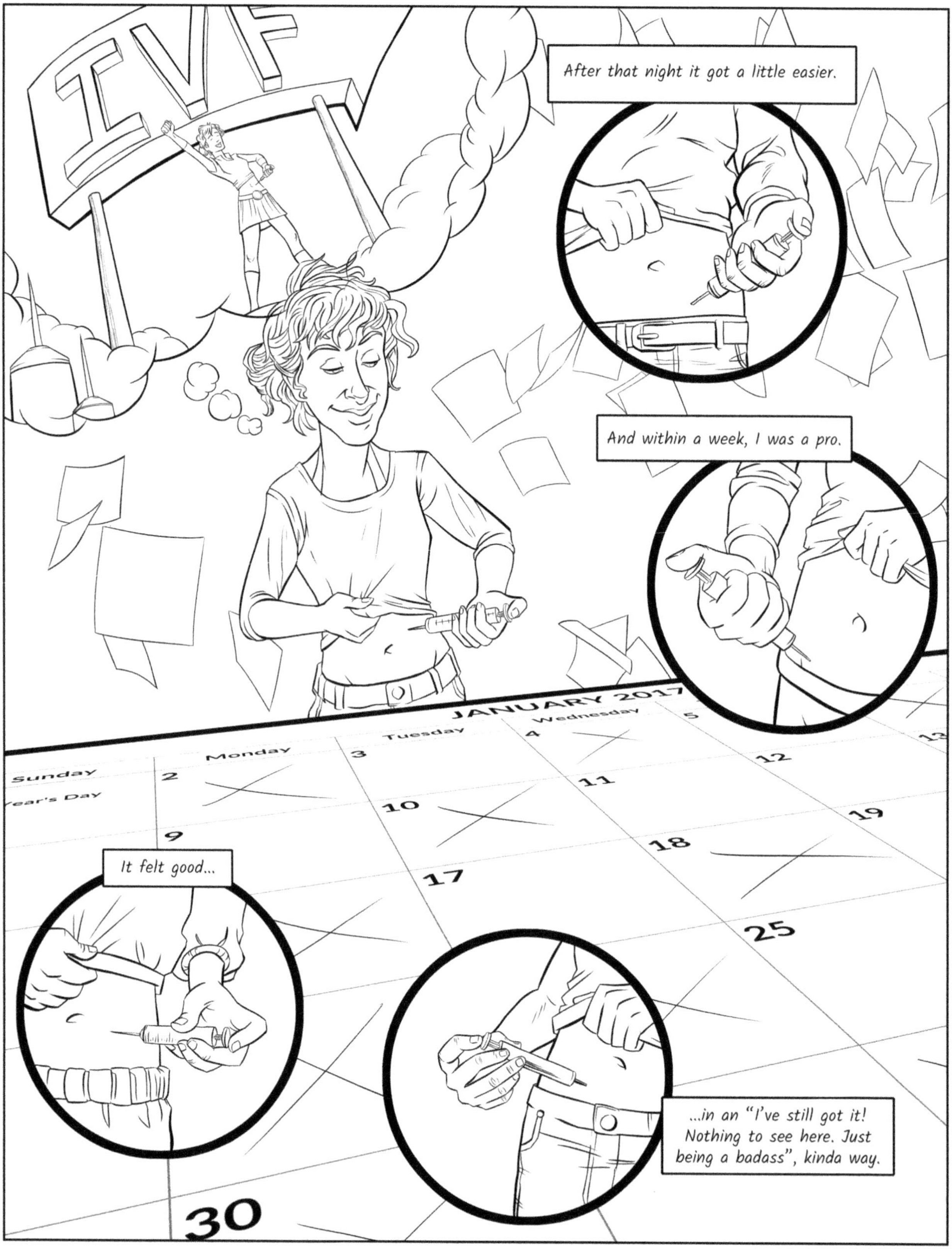

IVF
After that night it got a little easier.
And within a week, I was a pro.
JANUARY 2017
Sunday
Year's Day
Monday
Tuesday
Wednesday
It felt good...
...in an "I've still got it! Nothing to see here. Just being a badass", kinda way.

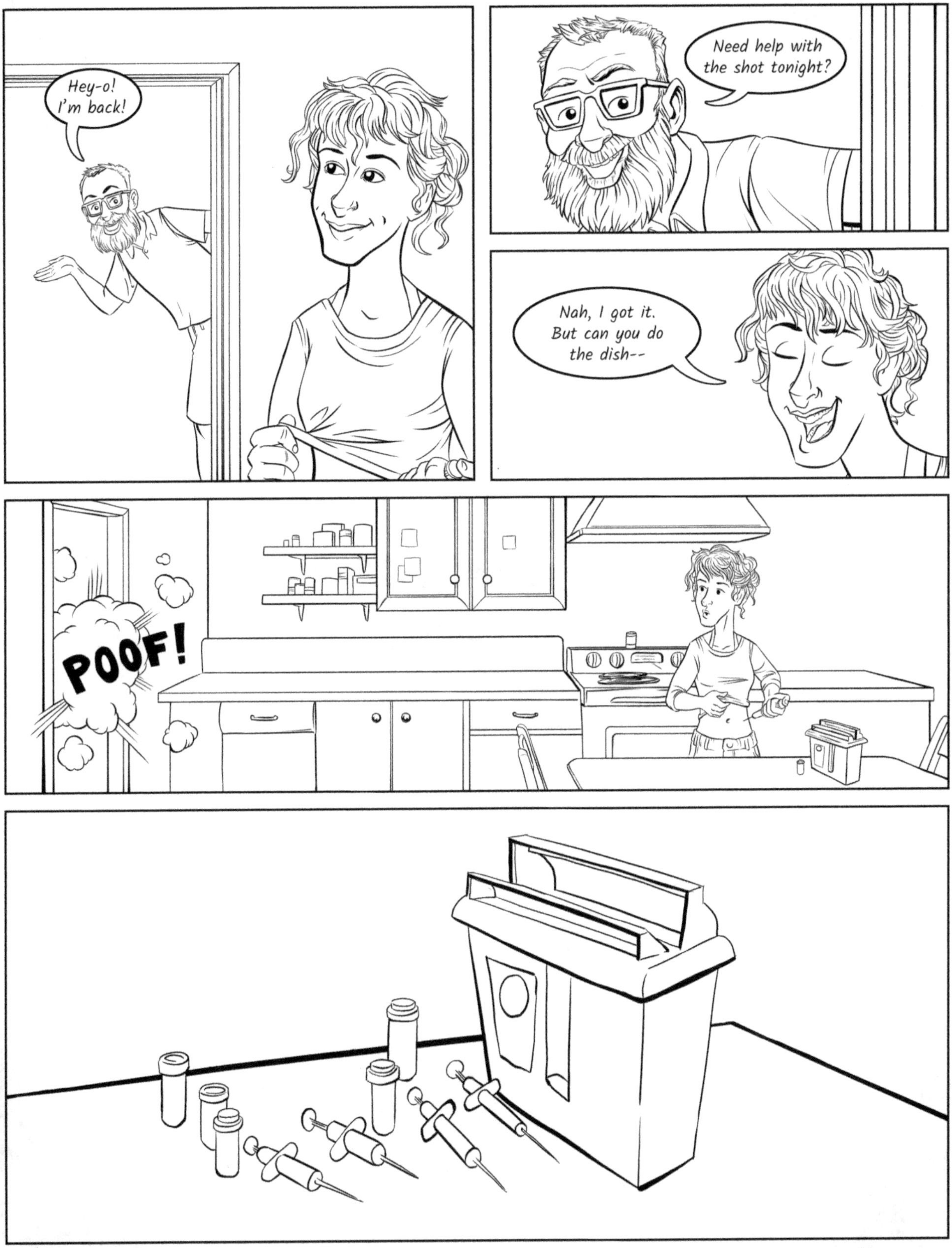
Hey-o!
I'm back!
Need help with the shot tonight?
Nah, I got it. But can you do the dish--
POOF!

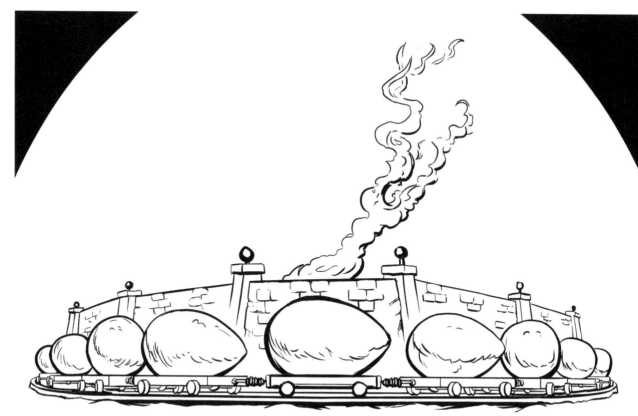

Feeling Like A Chicken

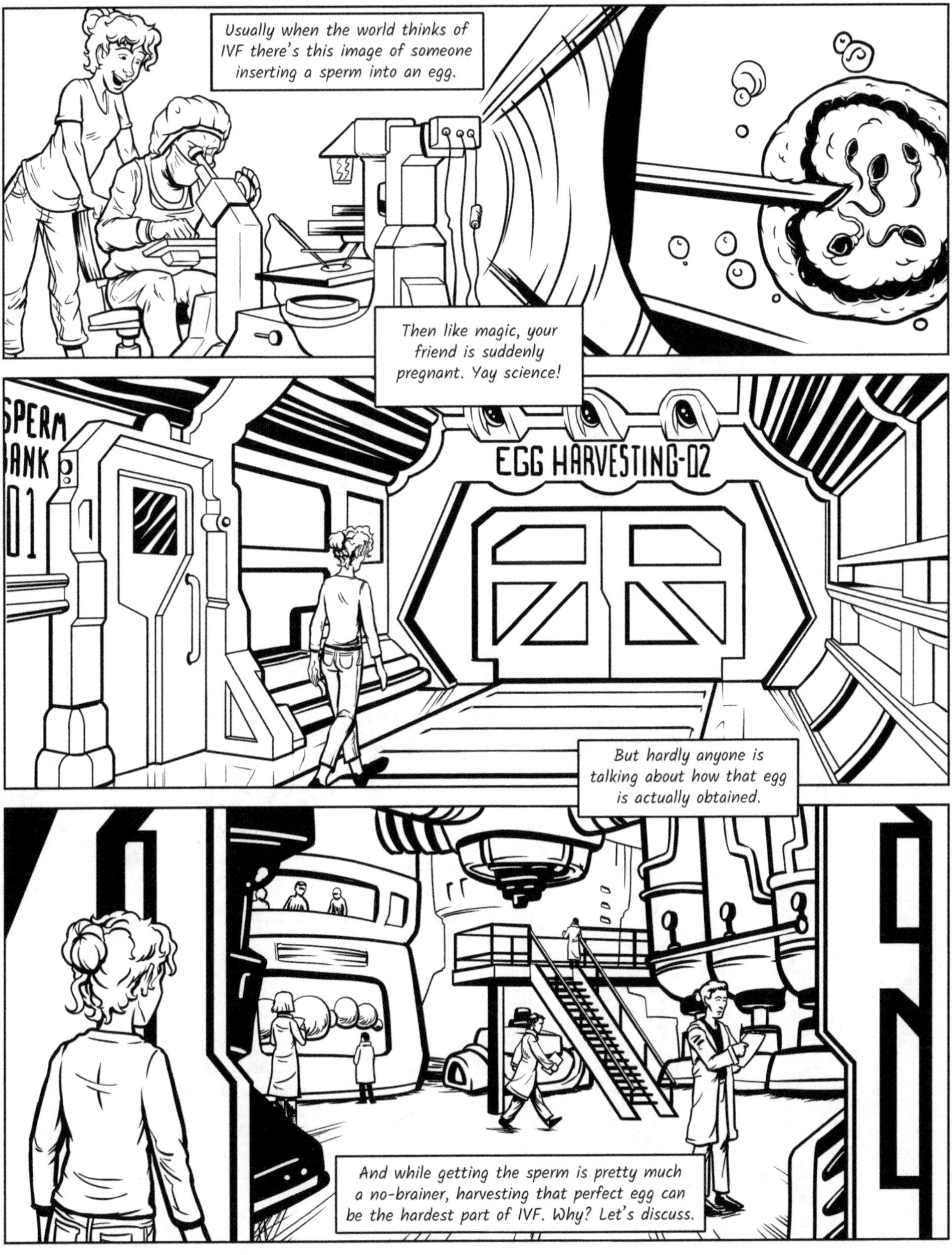
Usually when the world thinks of IVF there's this image of someone inserting a sperm into an egg.
Then like magic, your friend is suddenly pregnant. Yay science!
SPERM BANK 01
EGG HARVESTING-02
But hardly anyone is talking about how that egg is actually obtained.
And while getting the sperm is pretty much a no-brainer, harvesting that perfect egg can be the hardest part of IVF. Why? Let's discuss.

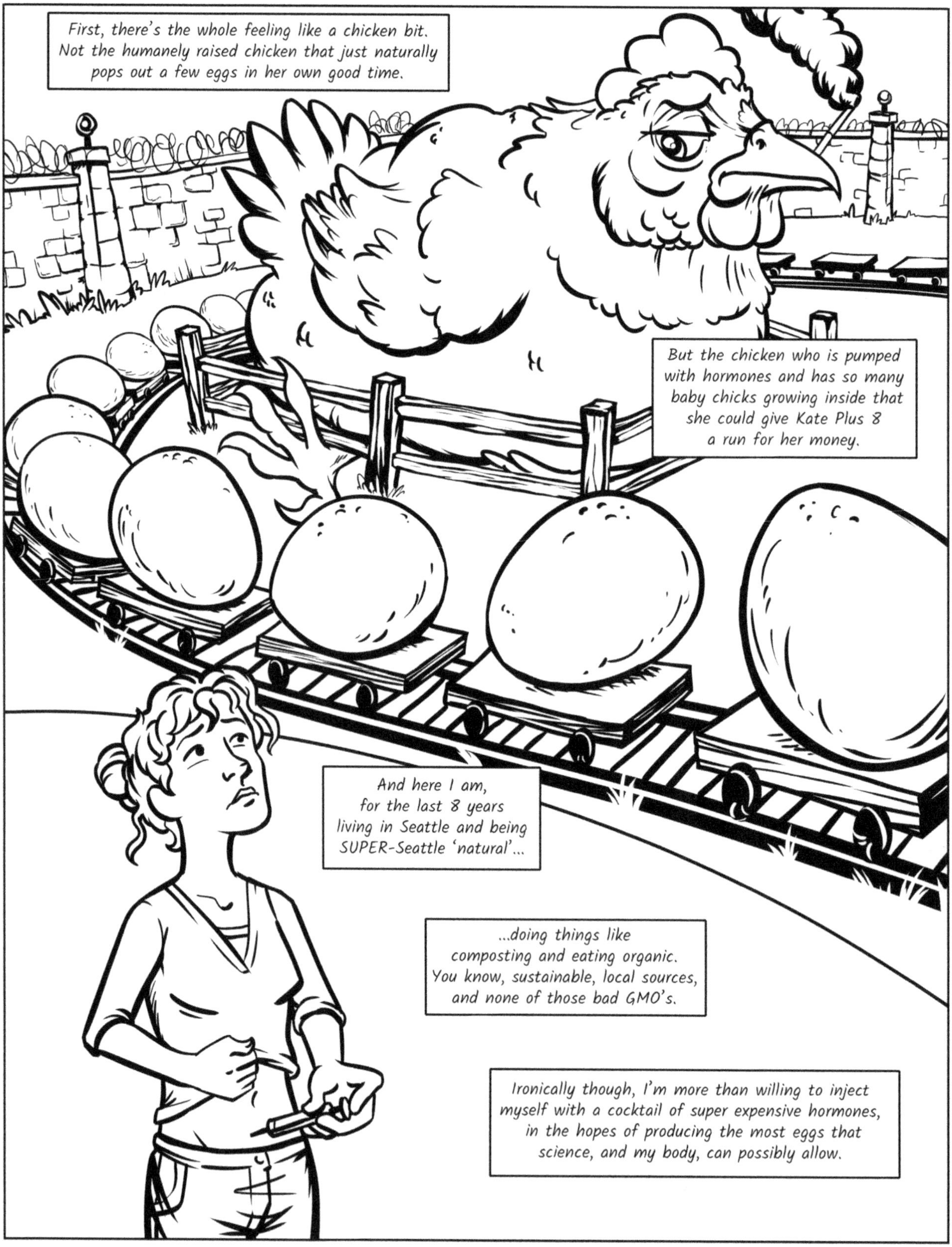
First, there's the whole feeling like a chicken bit. Not the humanely raised chicken that just naturally pops out a few eggs in her own good time.
But the chicken who is pumped with hormones and has so many baby chicks growing inside that she could give Kate Plus 8 a run for her money.
And here I am, for the last 8 years living in Seattle and being SUPER-Seattle 'natural'...
...doing things like composting and eating organic. You know, sustainable, local sources, and none of those bad GMO's.
Ironically though, I'm more than willing to inject myself with a cocktail of super expensive hormones, in the hopes of producing the most eggs that science, and my body, can possibly allow.

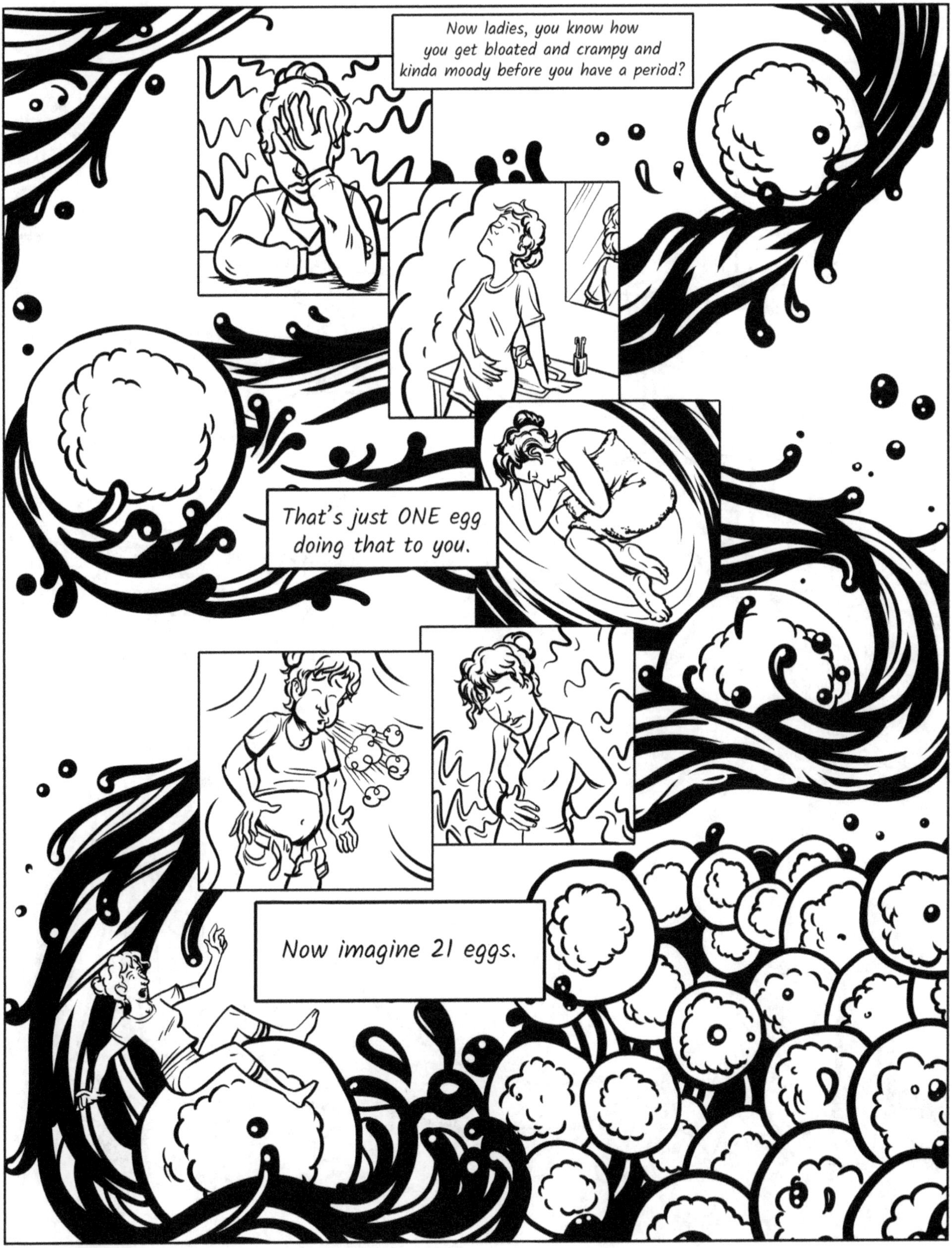
Now ladies, you know how you get bloated and crampy and kinda moody before you have a period?
That's just ONE egg doing that to you.
Now imagine 21 eggs.

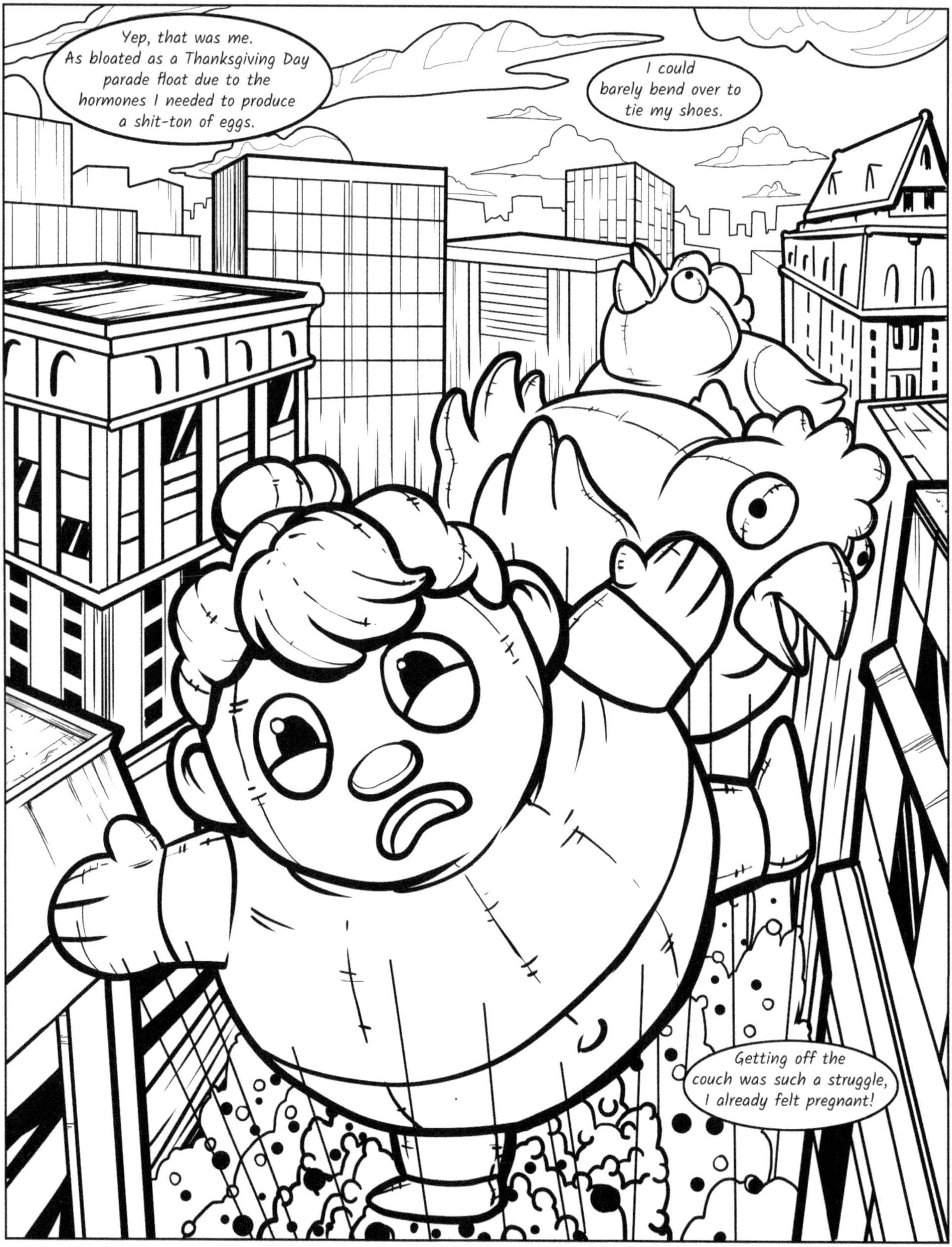
Yep, that was me. As bloated as a Thanksgiving Day parade float due to the hormones I needed to produce a shit-ton of eggs.
I could barely bend over to tie my shoes.
Getting off the couch was such a struggle, I already felt pregnant!

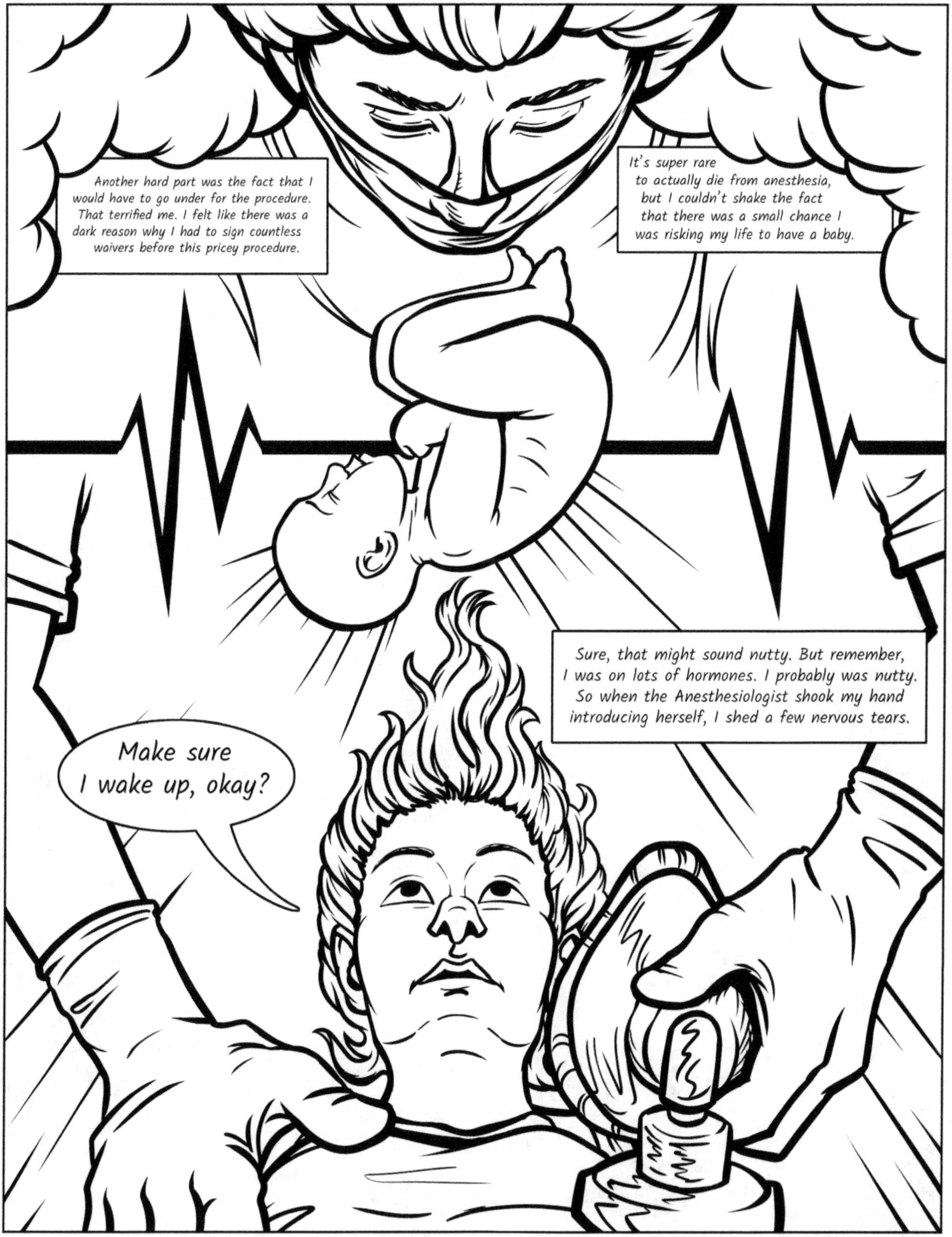
Another hard part was the fact that I would have to go under for the procedure. That terrified me. I felt like there was a dark reason why I had to sign countless waivers before this pricey procedure.
It's super rare to actually die from anesthesia, but I couldn't shake the fact that there was a small chance I was risking my life to have a baby.
Sure, that might sound nutty. But remember, I was on lots of hormones. I probably was nutty. So when the Anesthesiologist shook my hand introducing herself, I shed a few nervous tears.
Make sure I wake up, okay?

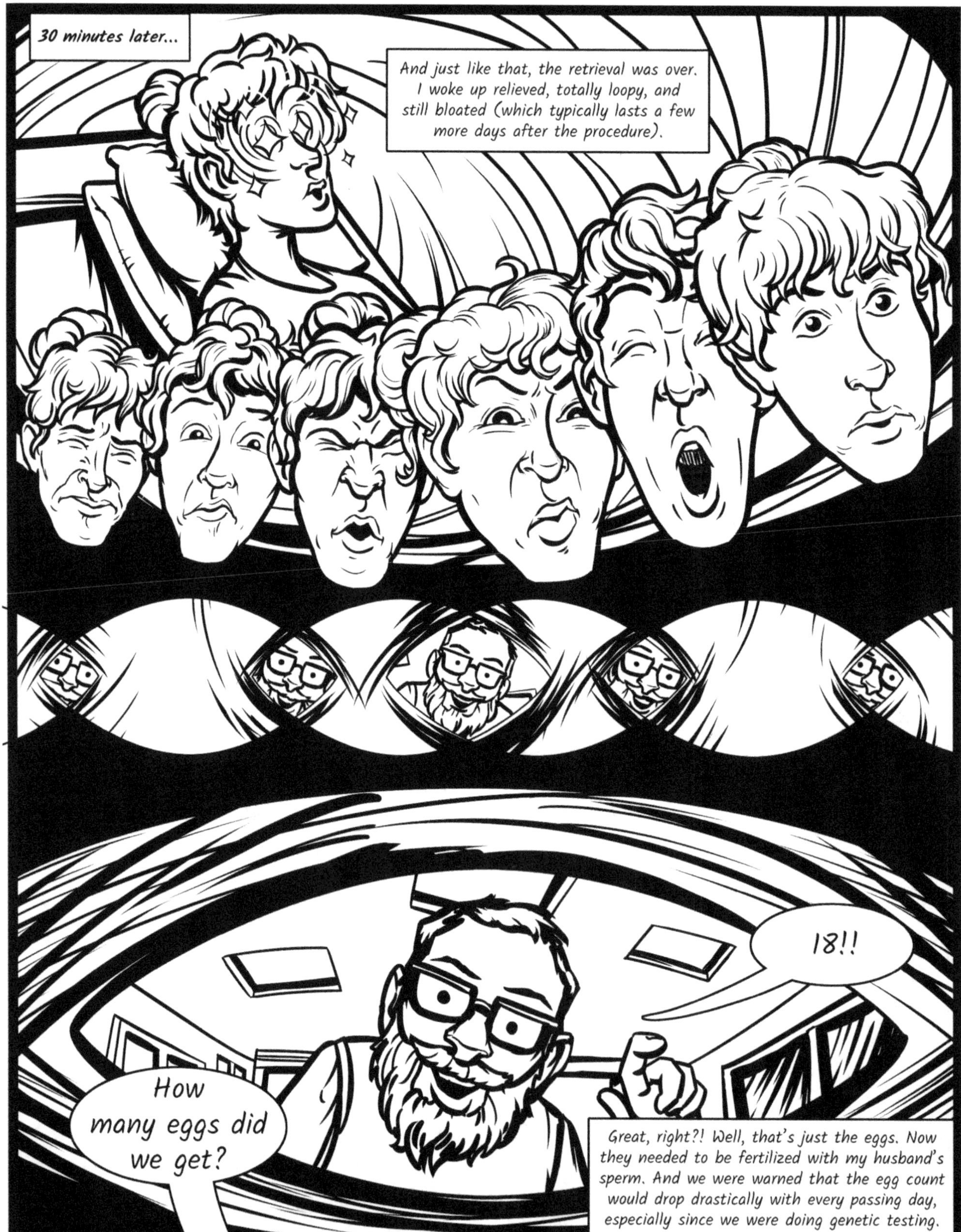
30 minutes later...
And just like that, the retrieval was over. I woke up relieved, totally loopy, and still bloated (which typically lasts a few more days after the procedure).
How many eggs did we get?
18!!
Great, right?! Well, that's just the eggs. Now they needed to be fertilized with my husband's sperm. And we were warned that the egg count would drop drastically with every passing day, especially since we were doing genetic testing.

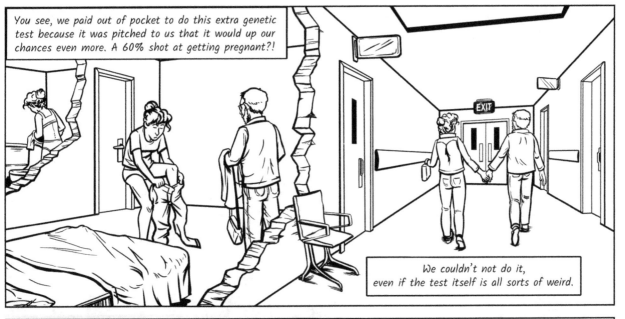

You see, we paid out of pocket to do this extra genetic test because it was pitched to us that it would up our chances even more. A 60% shot at getting pregnant?!

We couldn't not do it, even if the test itself is all sorts of weird.

Wait, what's so weird about genetic testing?

The short non-scientific answer is that someone in a lab coat takes a teeny tiny speck out of my cute little fertilized embryo and tests that speck for genetic diseases (it's usually these gene imperfections that, when undetected, end up causing someone to miscarry).

Supposedly taking bits out of an embryo doesn't affect the whole growing-to-be-a-perfect-baby thing. So we forked over $5k to ensure we would get grade A eggs.

And yes, fertility clinics actually grade them—just like chicken eggs.

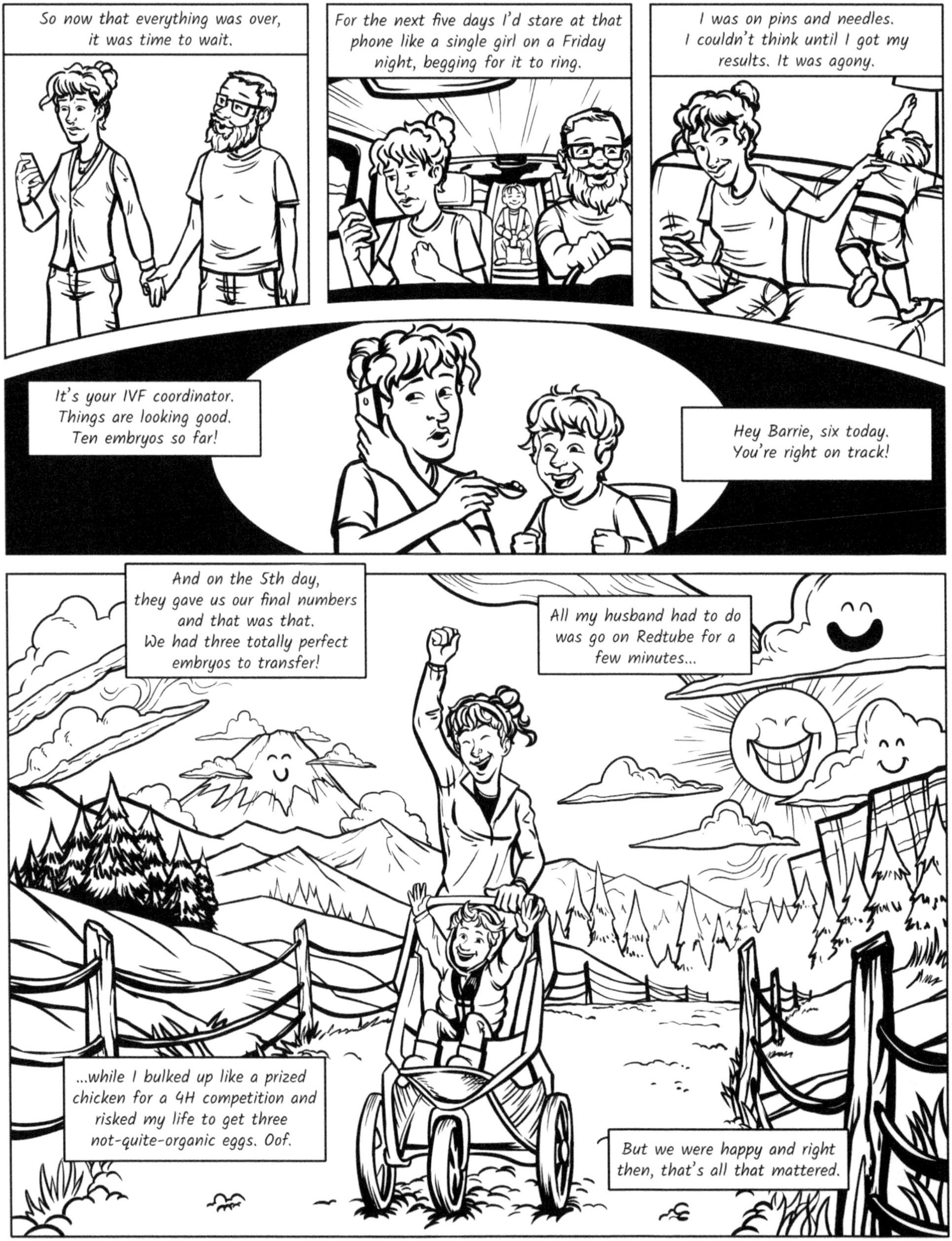
So now that everything was over, it was time to wait.
For the next five days I'd stare at that phone like a single girl on a Friday night, begging for it to ring.
I was on pins and needles. I couldn't think until I got my results. It was agony.
It's your IVF coordinator. Things are looking good. Ten embryos so far!
Hey Barrie, six today. You're right on track!
And on the 5th day, they gave us our final numbers and that was that. We had three totally perfect embryos to transfer!
All my husband had to do was go on Redtube for a few minutes...
...while I bulked up like a prized chicken for a 4H competition and risked my life to get three not-quite-organic eggs. Oof.
But we were happy and right then, that's all that mattered.

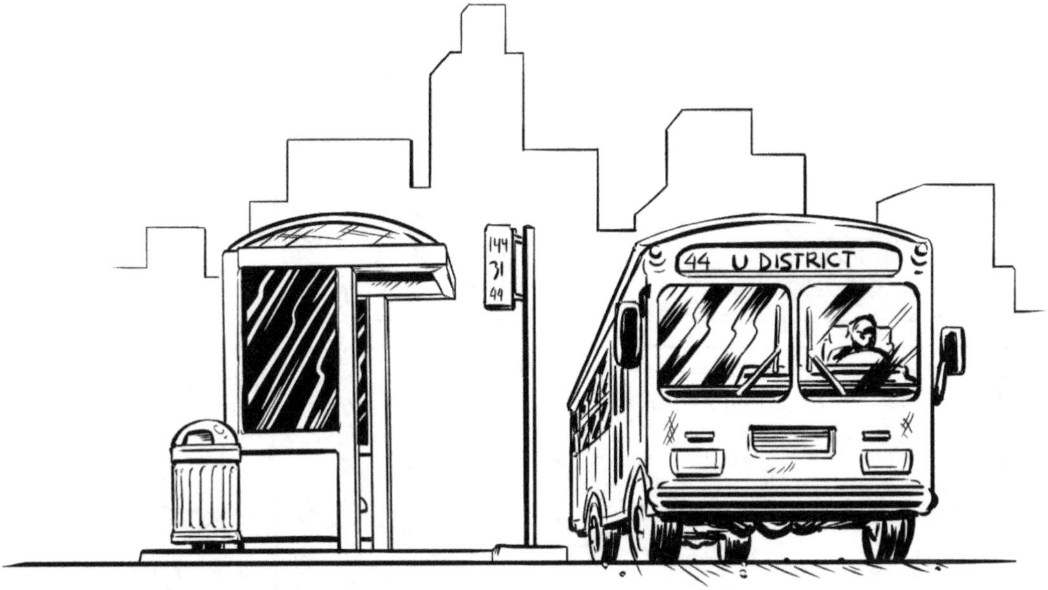
144
31
44
44 U DISTRICT

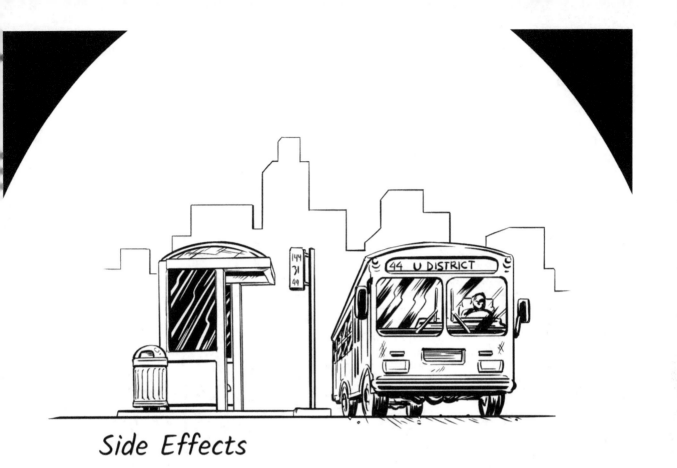

Side Effects

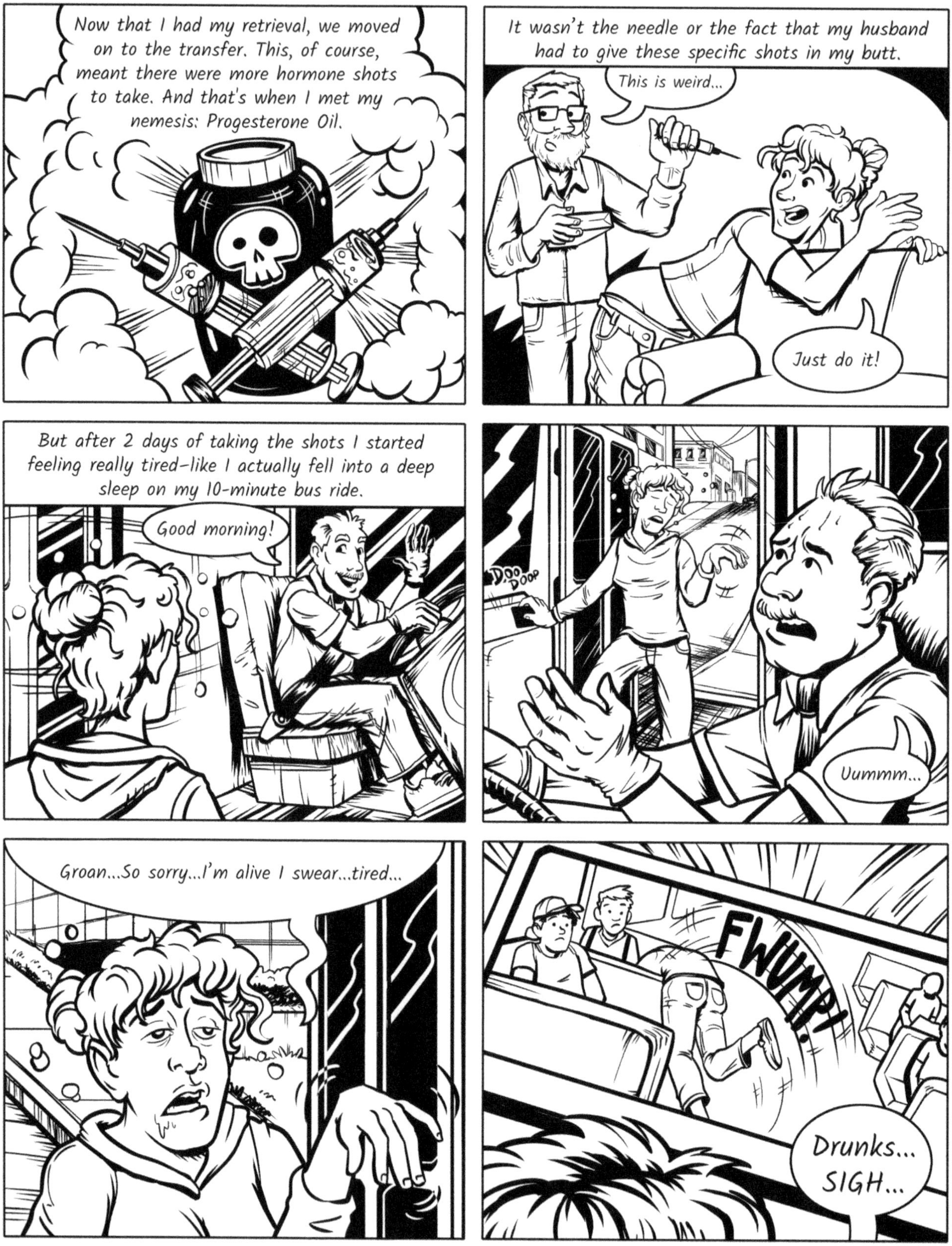
Now that I had my retrieval, we moved on to the transfer. This, of course, meant there were more hormone shots to take. And that's when I met my nemesis: Progesterone Oil.
It wasn't the needle or the fact that my husband had to give these specific shots in my butt.
This is weird...
Just do it!
But after 2 days of taking the shots I started feeling really tired–like I actually fell into a deep sleep on my 10-minute bus ride.
Good morning!
DOO DOOP
Uummm...
Groan...So sorry...I'm alive I swear...tired...
FWUMP!
Drunks... SIGH...

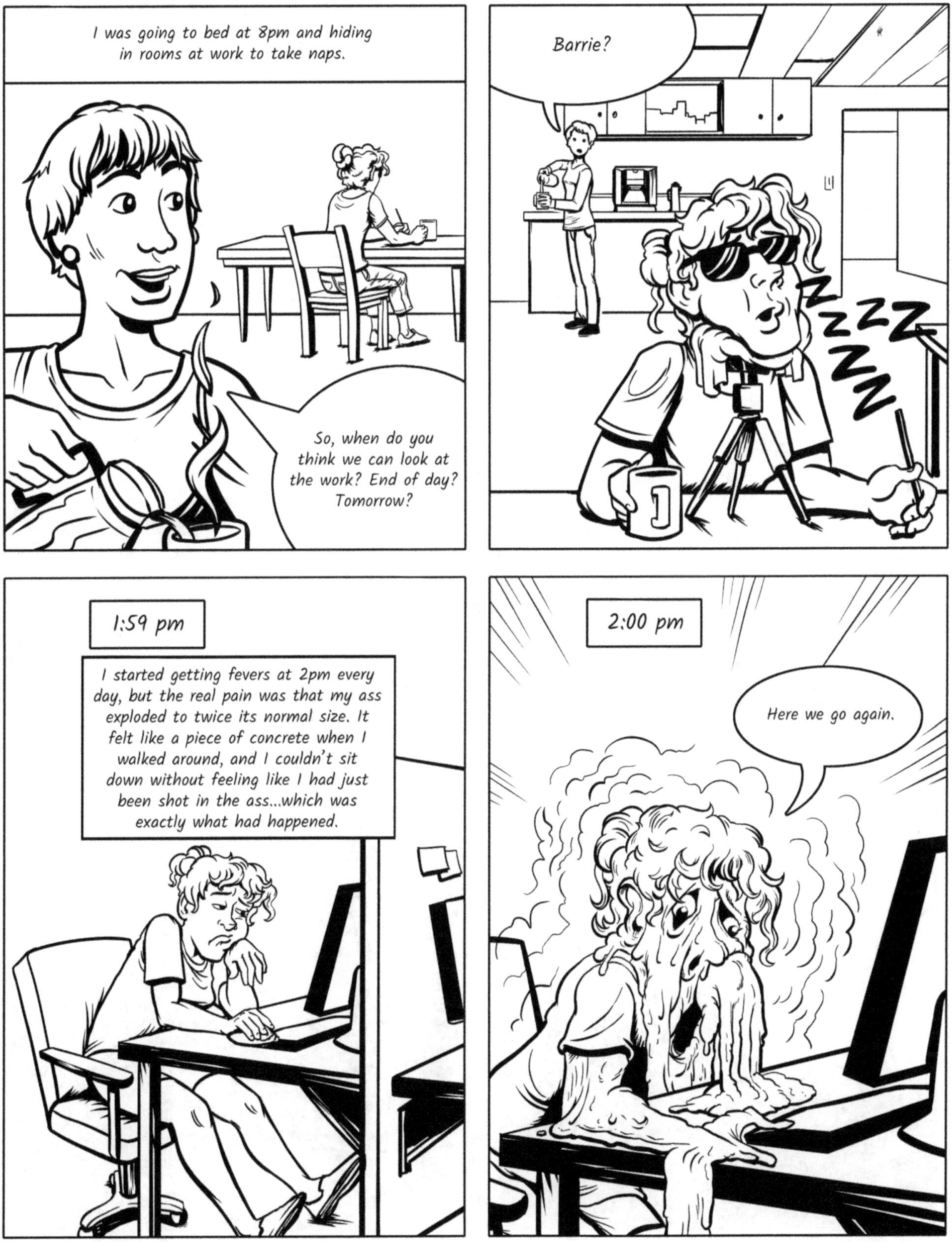
I was going to bed at 8pm and hiding in rooms at work to take naps.
So, when do you think we can look at the work? End of day? Tomorrow?
Barrie?
1:59 pm
I started getting fevers at 2pm every day, but the real pain was that my ass exploded to twice its normal size. It felt like a piece of concrete when I walked around, and I couldn't sit down without feeling like I had just been shot in the ass...which was exactly what had happened.
2:00 pm
Here we go again.

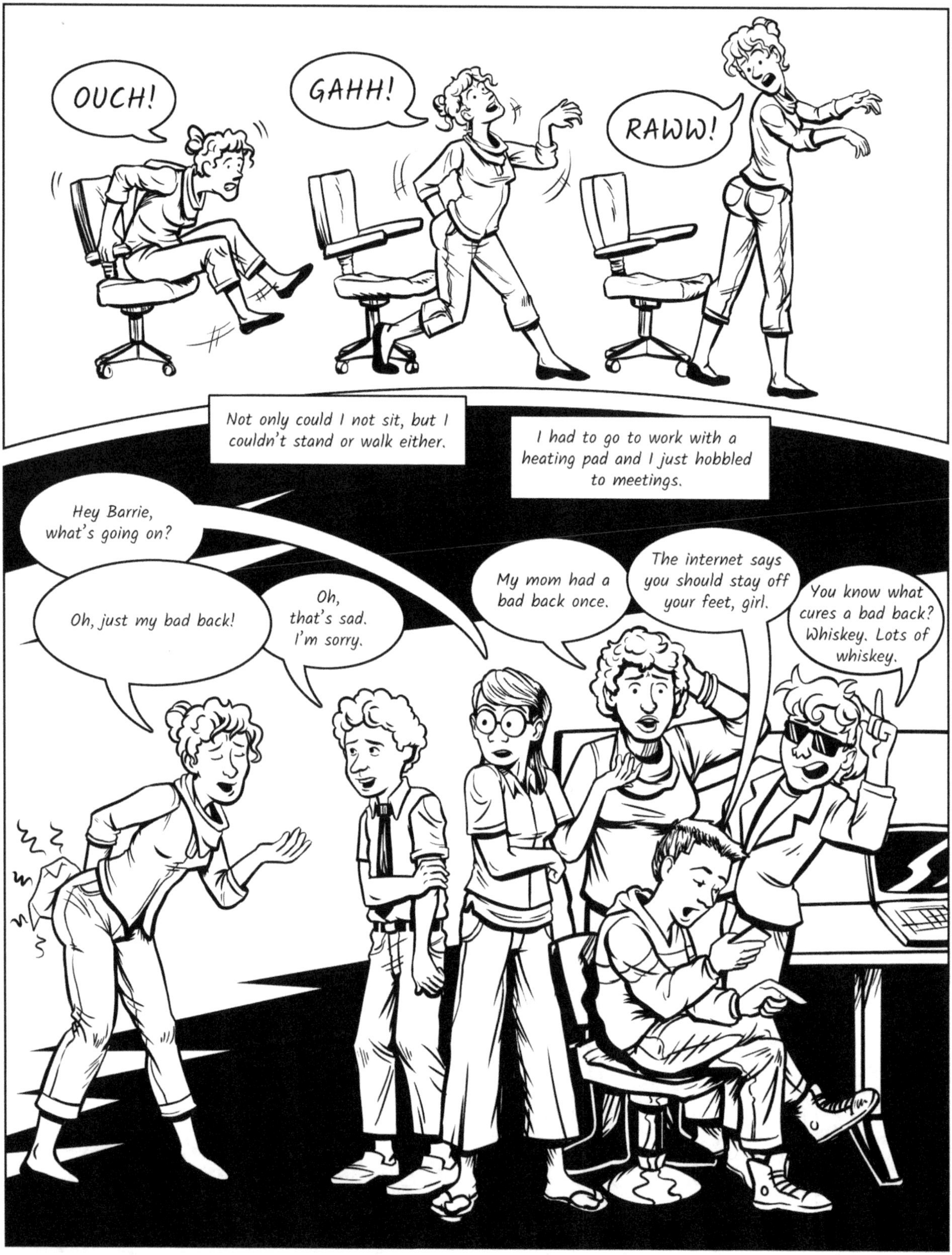
OUCH!
GAHH!
RAWW!
Not only could I not sit, but I couldn't stand or walk either.
I had to go to work with a heating pad and I just hobbled to meetings.
Hey Barrie, what's going on?
Oh, just my bad back!
Oh, that's sad. I'm sorry.
My mom had a bad back once.
The internet says you should stay off your feet, girl.
You know what cures a bad back? Whiskey. Lots of whiskey.

I was a week away from my very first transfer, when my RE said I'd have to keep doing these shots for another FOURTEEN WEEKS if I actually got pregnant. That's when I broke down.

I can't keep doing this. I can't walk. I can't stay awake. I can't regulate my body temperature. I can't fit into my pants.

Stopping the Progesterone Oil is a big risk. It could potentially hurt your chances of a successful transfer because...

ZZZZZZZZZZZZ

NUDGE NUDGE

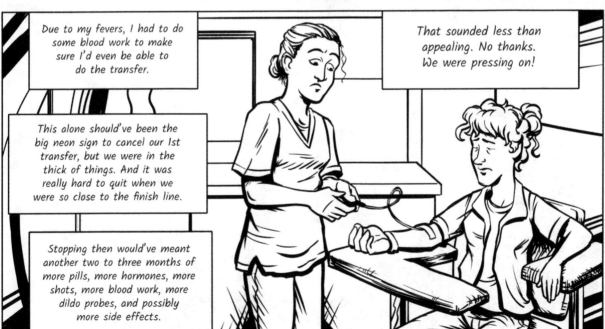

Due to my fevers, I had to do some blood work to make sure I'd even be able to do the transfer.

That sounded less than appealing. No thanks. We were pressing on!

This alone should've been the big neon sign to cancel our 1st transfer, but we were in the thick of things. And it was really hard to quit when we were so close to the finish line.

Stopping then would've meant another two to three months of more pills, more hormones, more shots, more blood work, more dildo probes, and possibly more side effects.

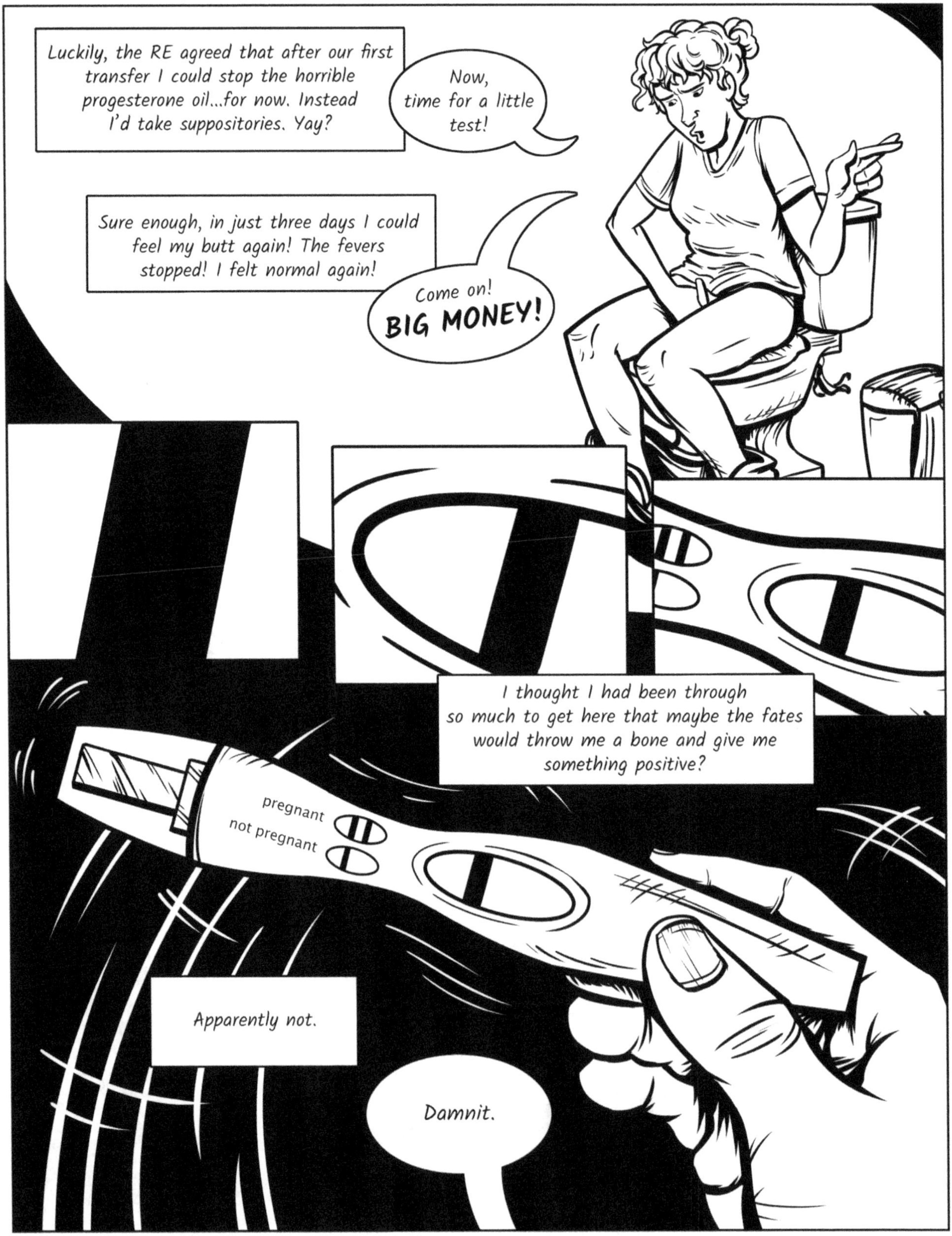
Luckily, the RE agreed that after our first transfer I could stop the horrible progesterone oil...for now. Instead I'd take suppositories. Yay?
Now, time for a little test!
Sure enough, in just three days I could feel my butt again! The fevers stopped! I felt normal again!
Come on! BIG MONEY!
I thought I had been through so much to get here that maybe the fates would throw me a bone and give me something positive?
pregnant
not pregnant
Apparently not.
Damnit.

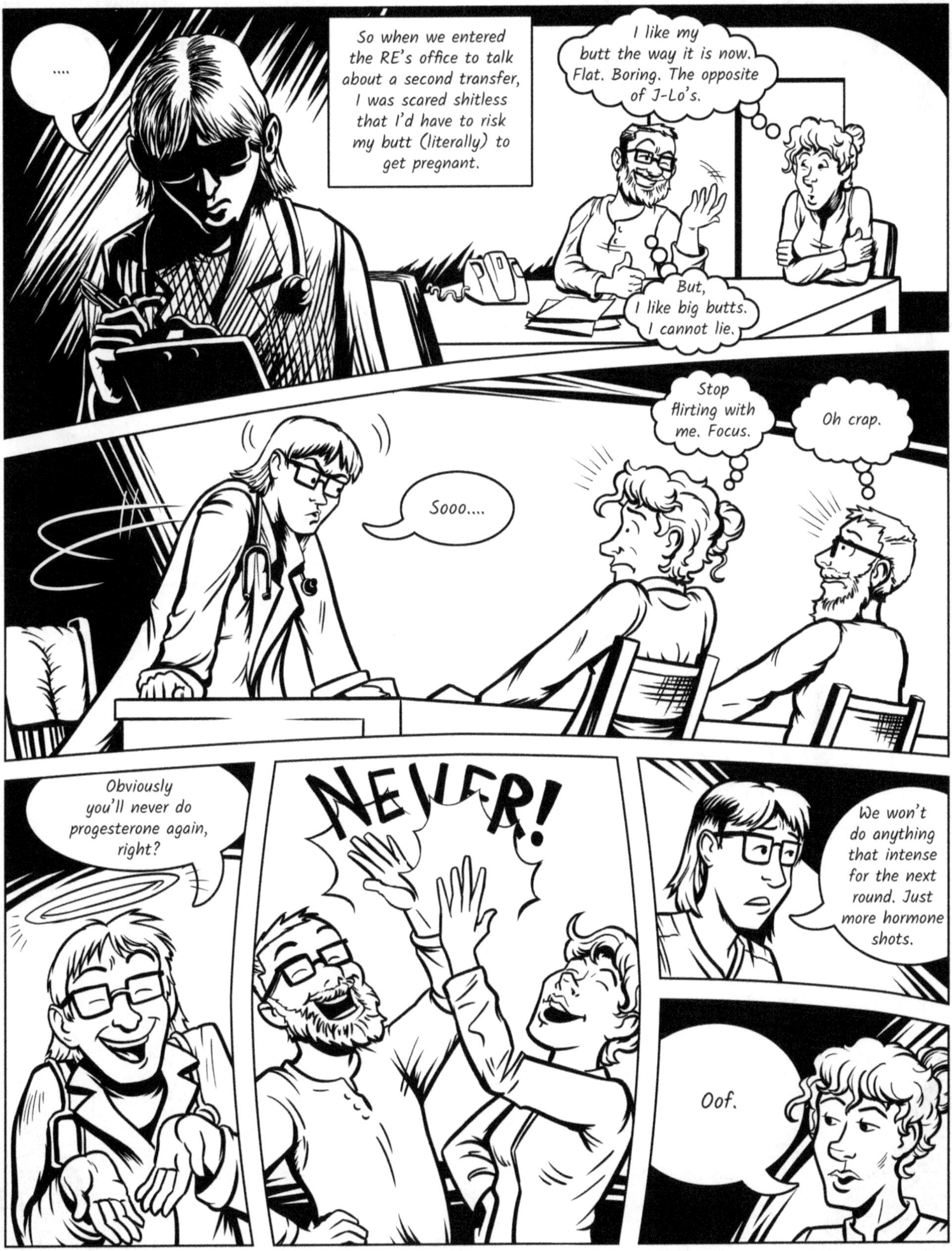
....
So when we entered the RE's office to talk about a second transfer, I was scared shitless that I'd have to risk my butt (literally) to get pregnant.
I like my butt the way it is now. Flat. Boring. The opposite of J-Lo's.
But, I like big butts. I cannot lie.
Stop flirting with me. Focus.
Oh crap.
Sooo....
Obviously you'll never do progesterone again, right?
NEVER!
We won't do anything that intense for the next round. Just more hormone shots.
Oof.

Motherfucking Insurance Company

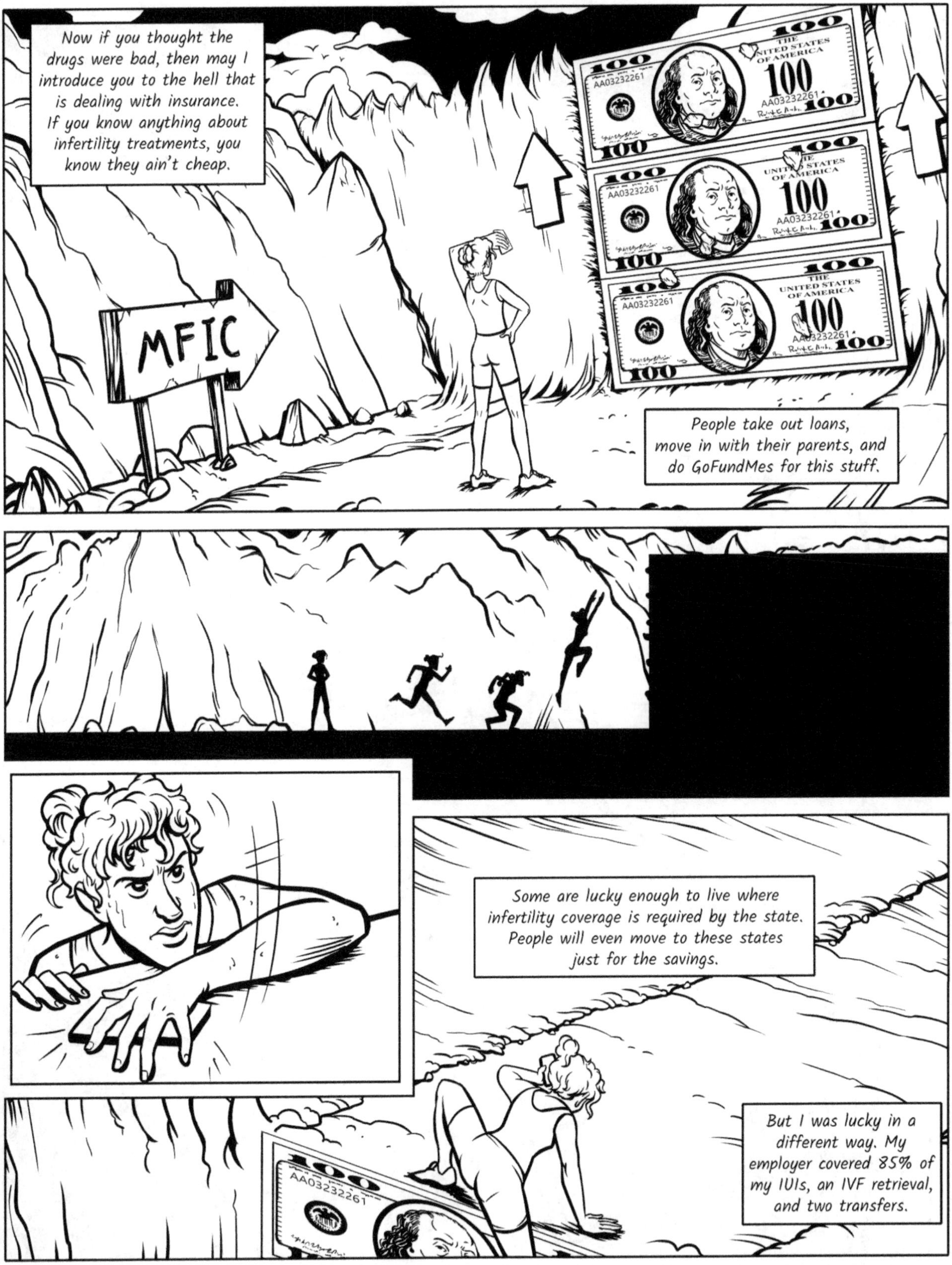
Now if you thought the drugs were bad, then may I introduce you to the hell that is dealing with insurance. If you know anything about infertility treatments, you know they ain't cheap.
MFIC
100
THE UNITED STATES OF AMERICA
AA03232261
People take out loans, move in with their parents, and do GoFundMes for this stuff.
Some are lucky enough to live where infertility coverage is required by the state. People will even move to these states just for the savings.
But I was lucky in a different way. My employer covered 85% of my IUIs, an IVF retrieval, and two transfers.

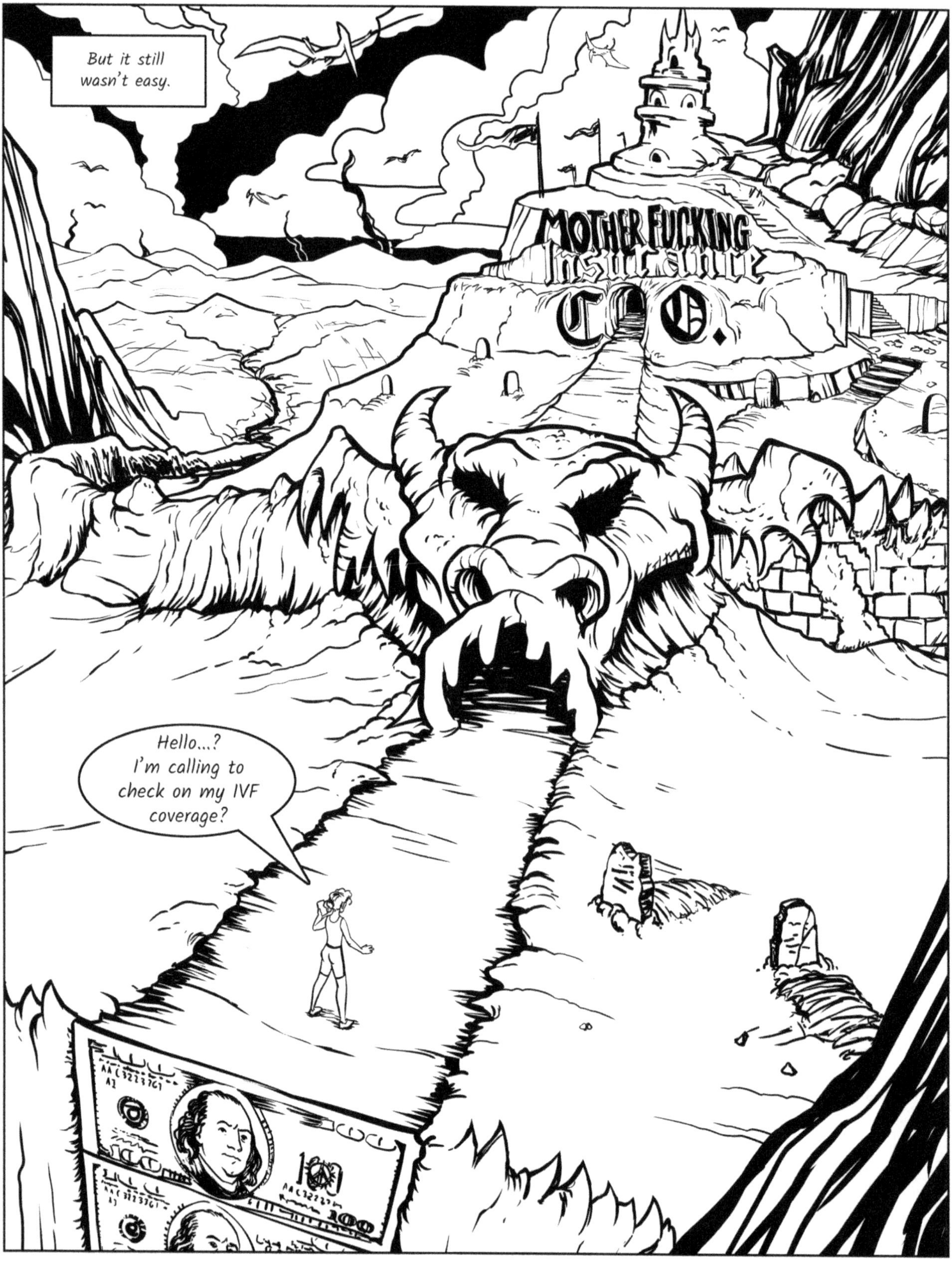
But it still wasn't easy.
MOTHER FUCKING
Insurance
CO.
Hello...? I'm calling to check on my IVF coverage?

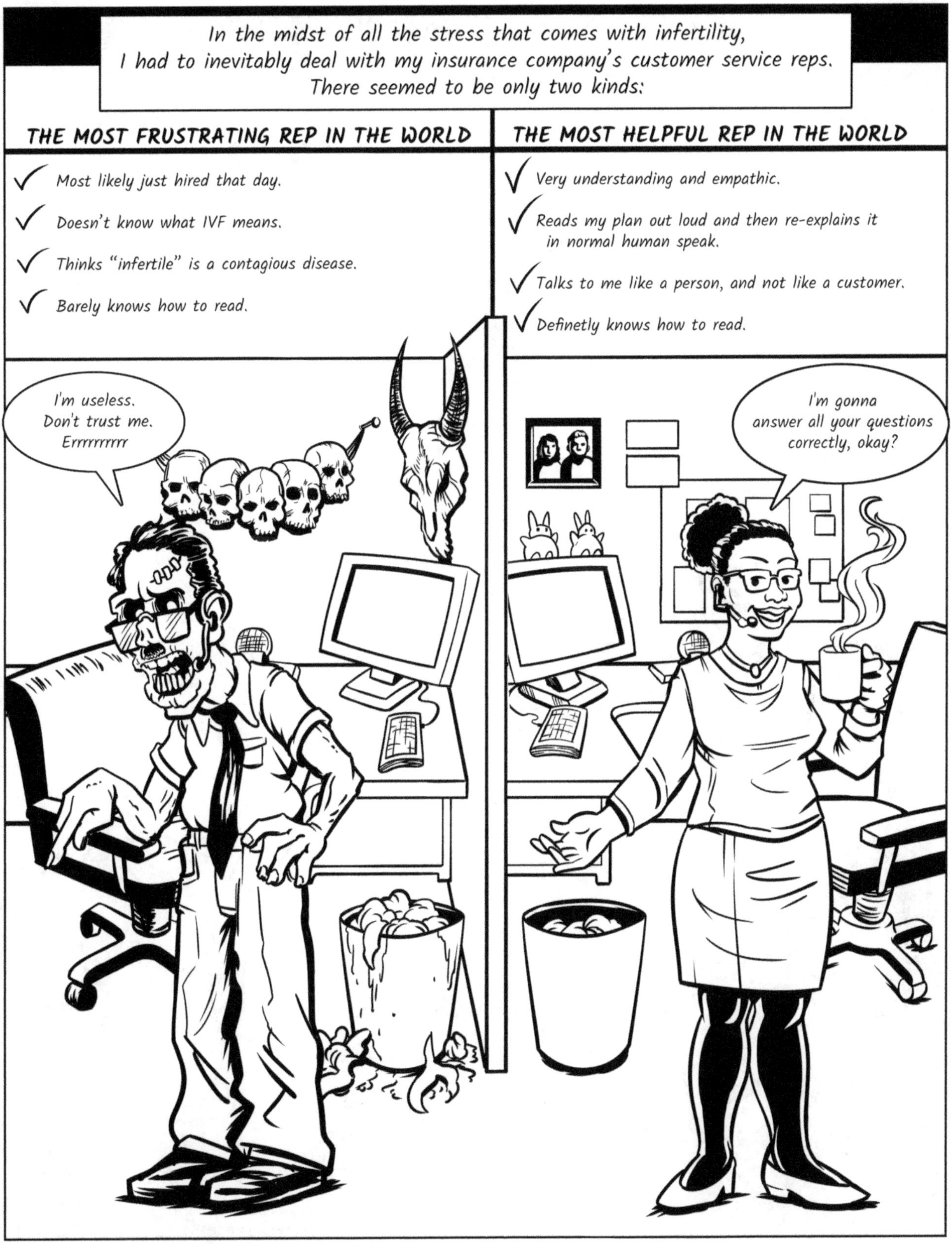
In the midst of all the stress that comes with infertility,
I had to inevitably deal with my insurance company's customer service reps.
There seemed to be only two kinds:
THE MOST FRUSTRATING REP IN THE WORLD
Most likely just hired that day.
Doesn't know what IVF means.
Thinks "infertile" is a contagious disease.
Barely knows how to read.
THE MOST HELPFUL REP IN THE WORLD
Very understanding and empathic.
Reads my plan out loud and then re-explains it in normal human speak.
Talks to me like a person, and not like a customer.
Definetly knows how to read.
I'm useless. Don't trust me. Errrrrrrrr
I'm gonna answer all your questions correctly, okay?

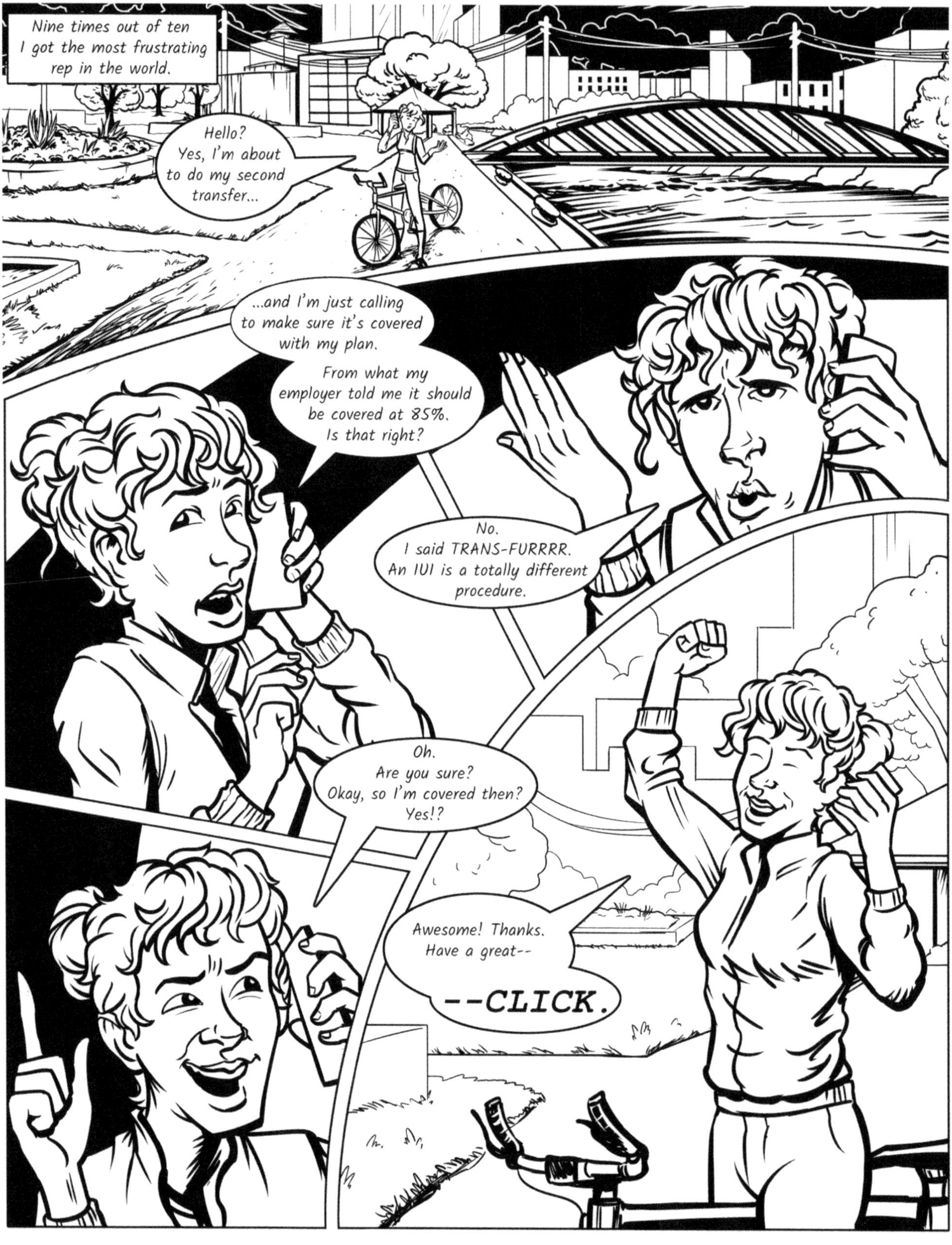
Nine times out of ten I got the most frustrating rep in the world.
Hello? Yes, I'm about to do my second transfer...
...and I'm just calling to make sure it's covered with my plan.
From what my employer told me it should be covered at 85%. Is that right?
No. I said TRANS-FURRRR. An IUI is a totally different procedure.
Oh. Are you sure? Okay, so I'm covered then? Yes!?
Awesome! Thanks. Have a great--
--CLICK.

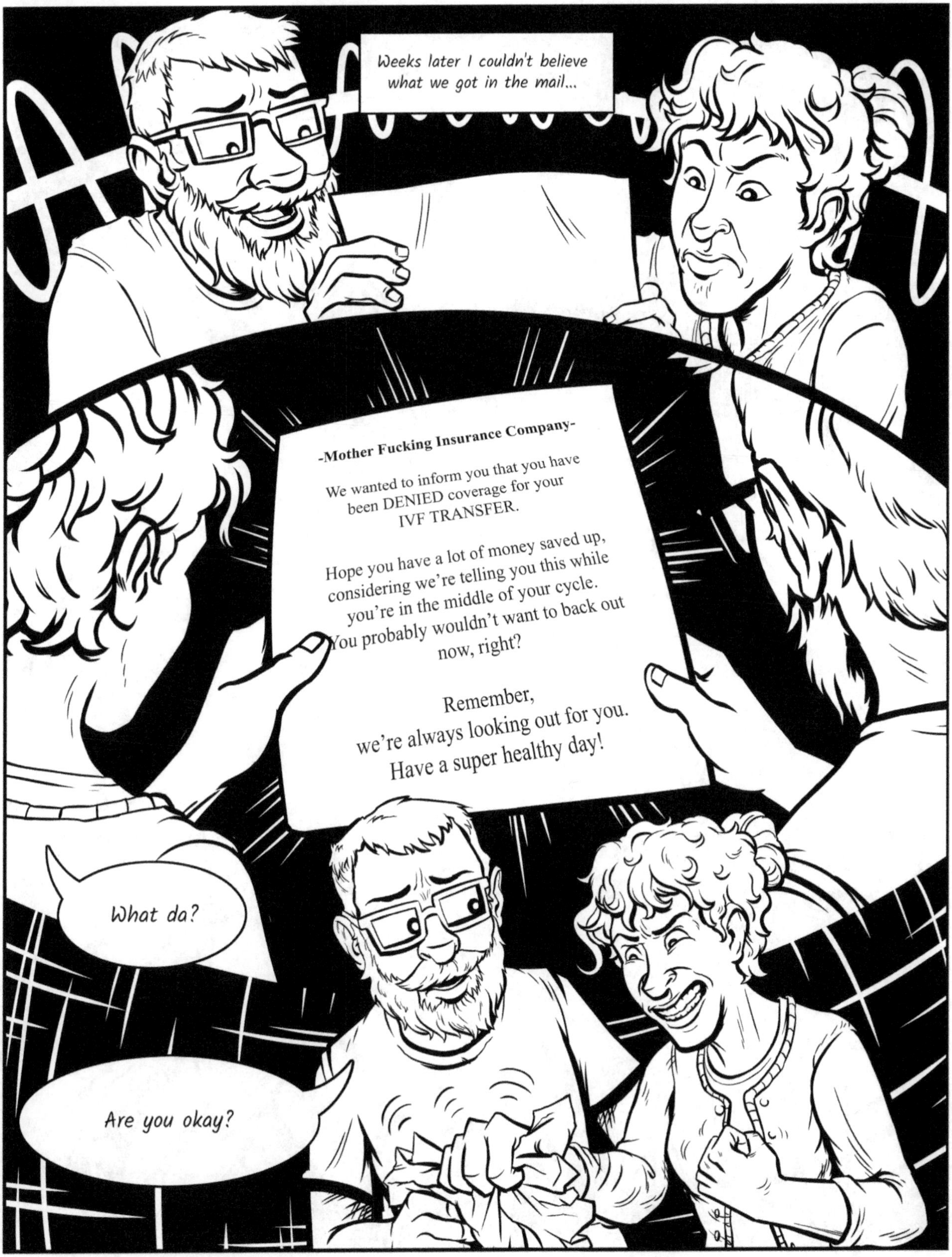
Weeks later I couldn't believe what we got in the mail...
-Mother Fucking Insurance Company-
We wanted to inform you that you have been DENIED coverage for your IVF TRANSFER.
Hope you have a lot of money saved up, considering we're telling you this while you're in the middle of your cycle. You probably wouldn't want to back out now, right?
Remember, we're always looking out for you. Have a super healthy day!
What da?
Are you okay?

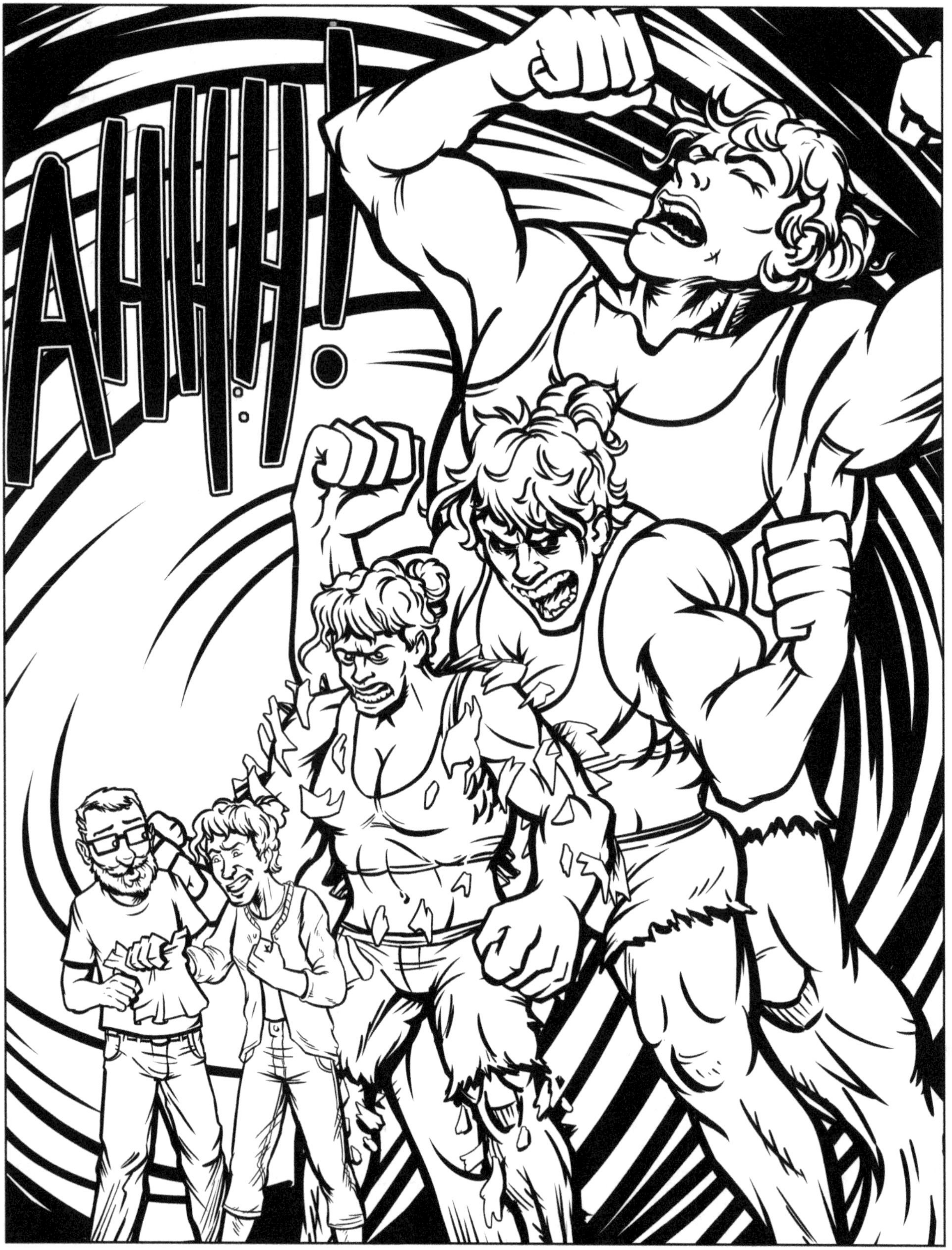
AHHH!

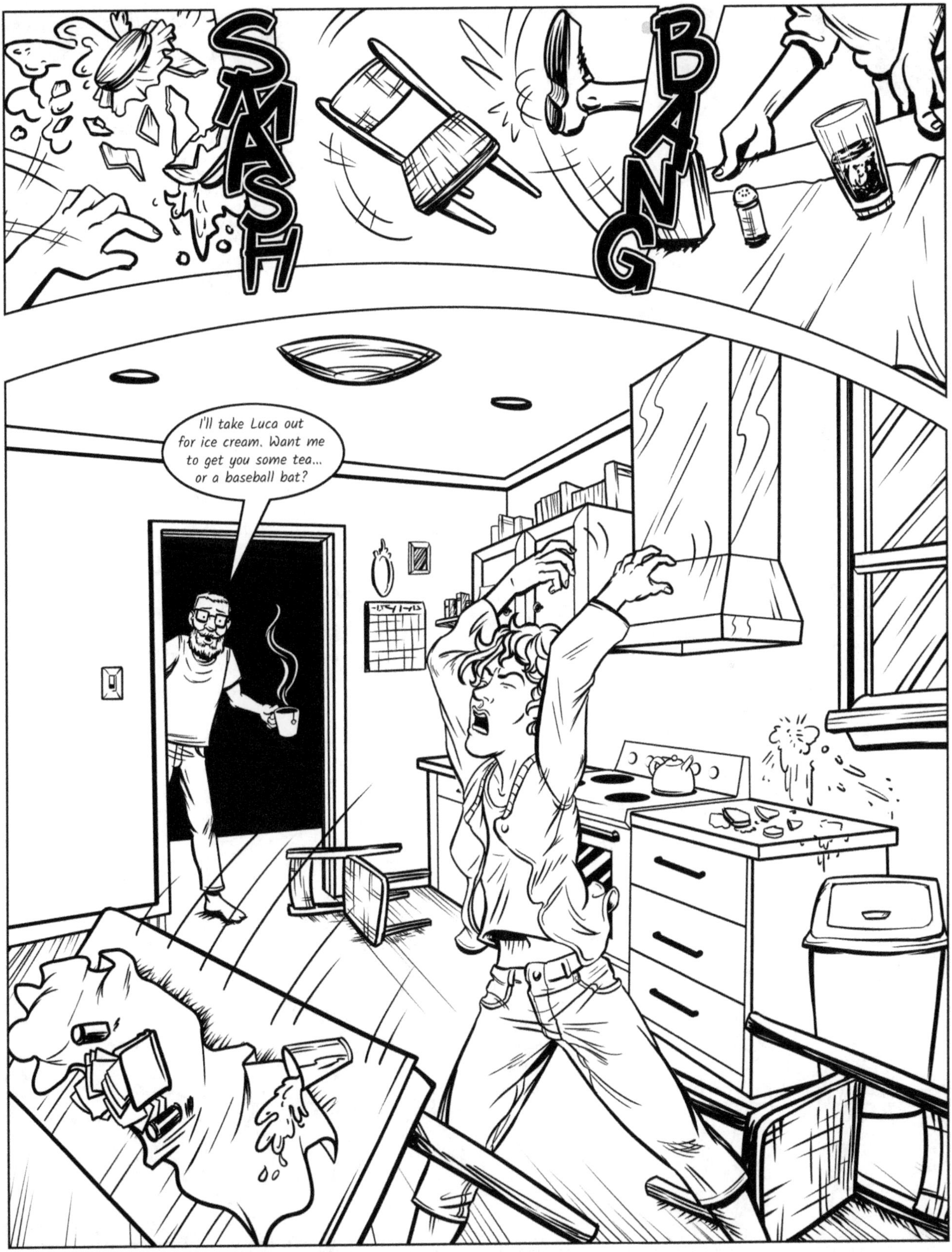
SMASH
BANG
I'll take Luca out for ice cream. Want me to get you some tea... or a baseball bat?

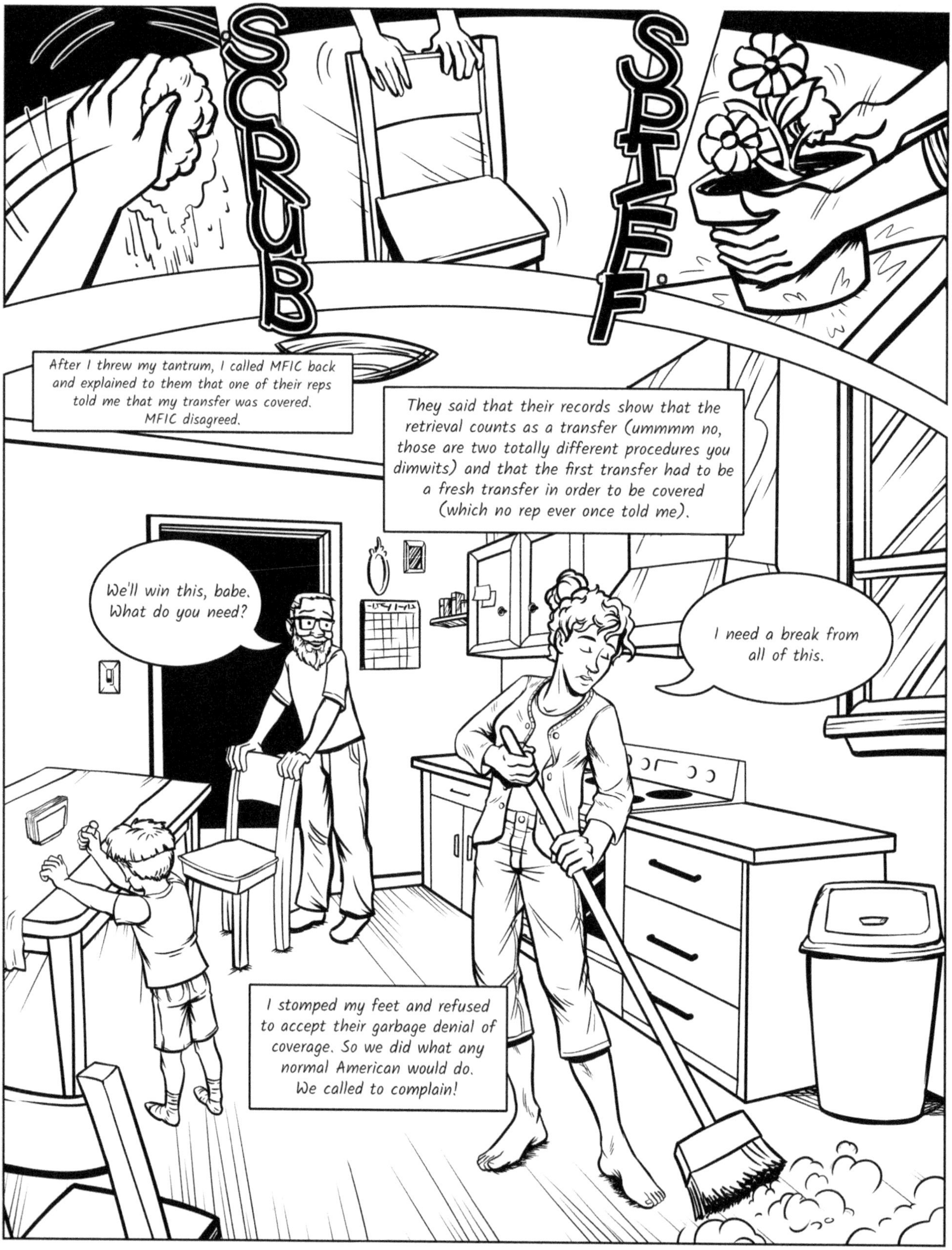
SCRUB
SPIFF
After I threw my tantrum, I called MFIC back and explained to them that one of their reps told me that my transfer was covered. MFIC disagreed.
They said that their records show that the retrieval counts as a transfer (ummmm no, those are two totally different procedures you dimwits) and that the first transfer had to be a fresh transfer in order to be covered (which no rep ever once told me).
We'll win this, babe. What do you need?
I need a break from all of this.
I stomped my feet and refused to accept their garbage denial of coverage. So we did what any normal American would do. We called to complain!

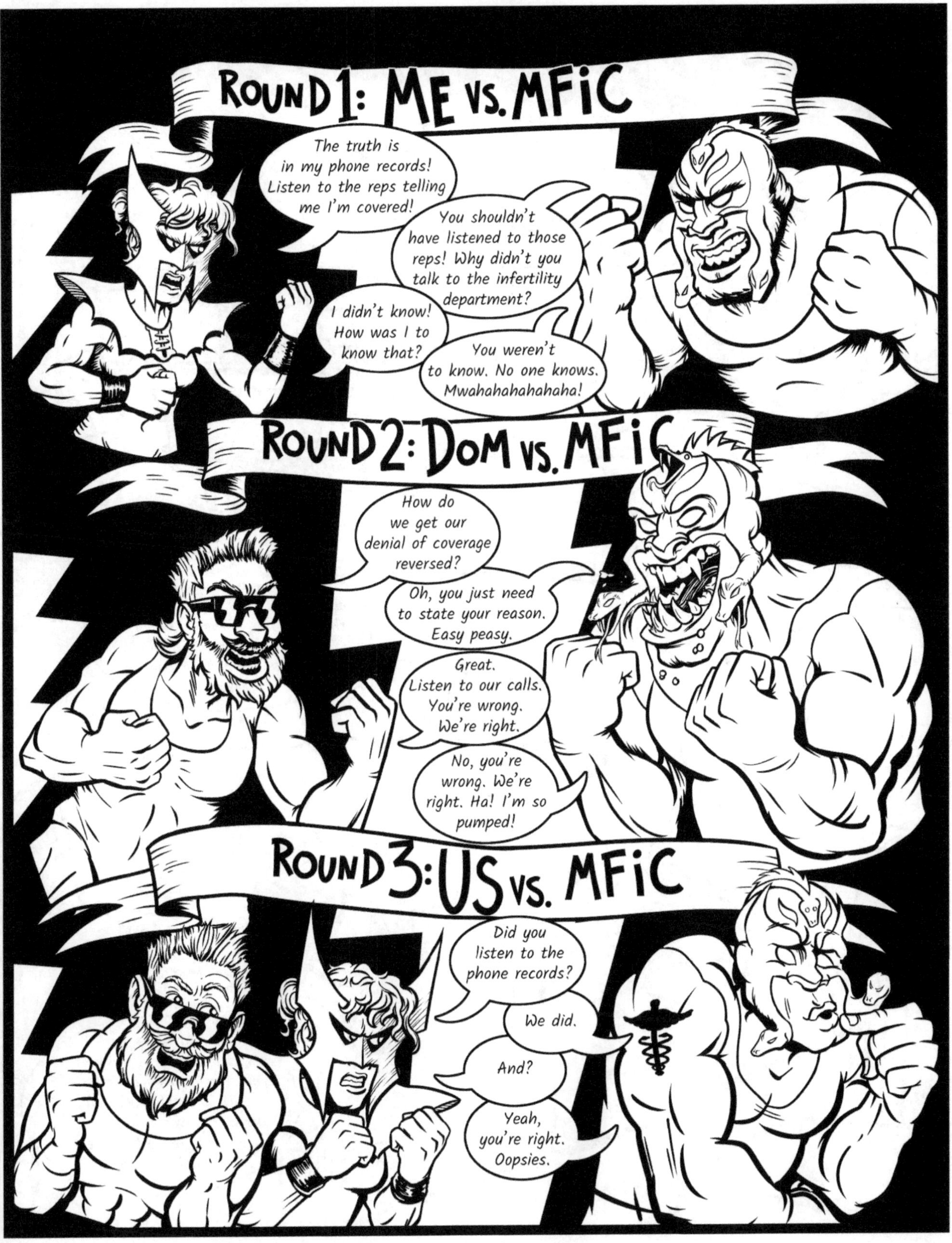
ROUND 1: ME VS. MFiC
The truth is in my phone records! Listen to the reps telling me I'm covered!
You shouldn't have listened to those reps! Why didn't you talk to the infertility department?
I didn't know! How was I to know that?
You weren't to know. No one knows. Mwahahahahahaha!
ROUND 2: DOM VS. MFiC
How do we get our denial of coverage reversed?
Oh, you just need to state your reason. Easy peasy.
Great. Listen to our calls. You're wrong. We're right.
No, you're wrong. We're right. Ha! I'm so pumped!
ROUND 3: US VS. MFiC
Did you listen to the phone records?
We did.
And?
Yeah, you're right. Oopsies.

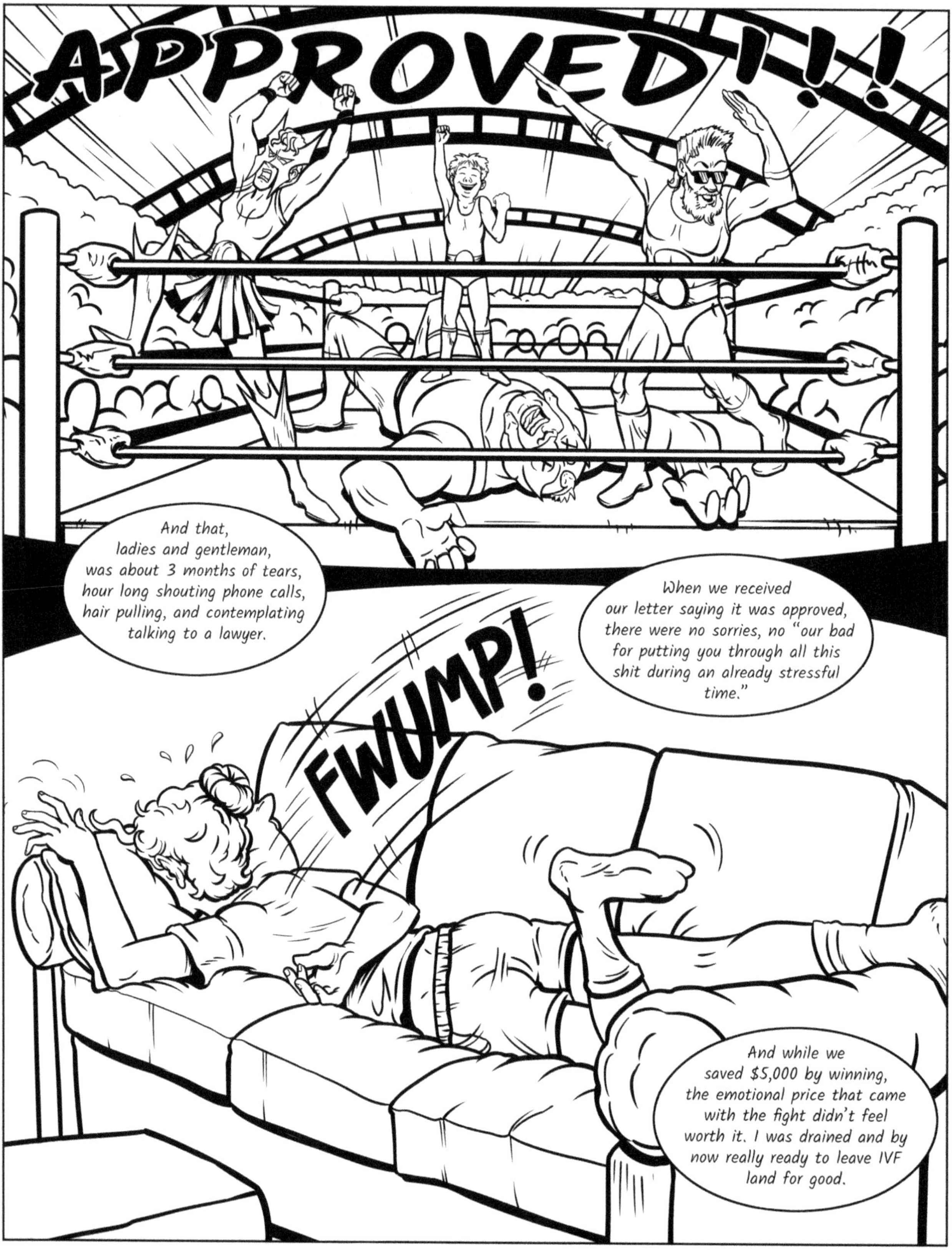
APPROVED!!!
And that, ladies and gentleman, was about 3 months of tears, hour long shouting phone calls, hair pulling, and contemplating talking to a lawyer.
When we received our letter saying it was approved, there were no sorries, no "our bad for putting you through all this shit during an already stressful time."
FWUMP!
And while we saved $5,000 by winning, the emotional price that came with the fight didn't feel worth it. I was drained and by now really ready to leave IVF land for good.

The End?

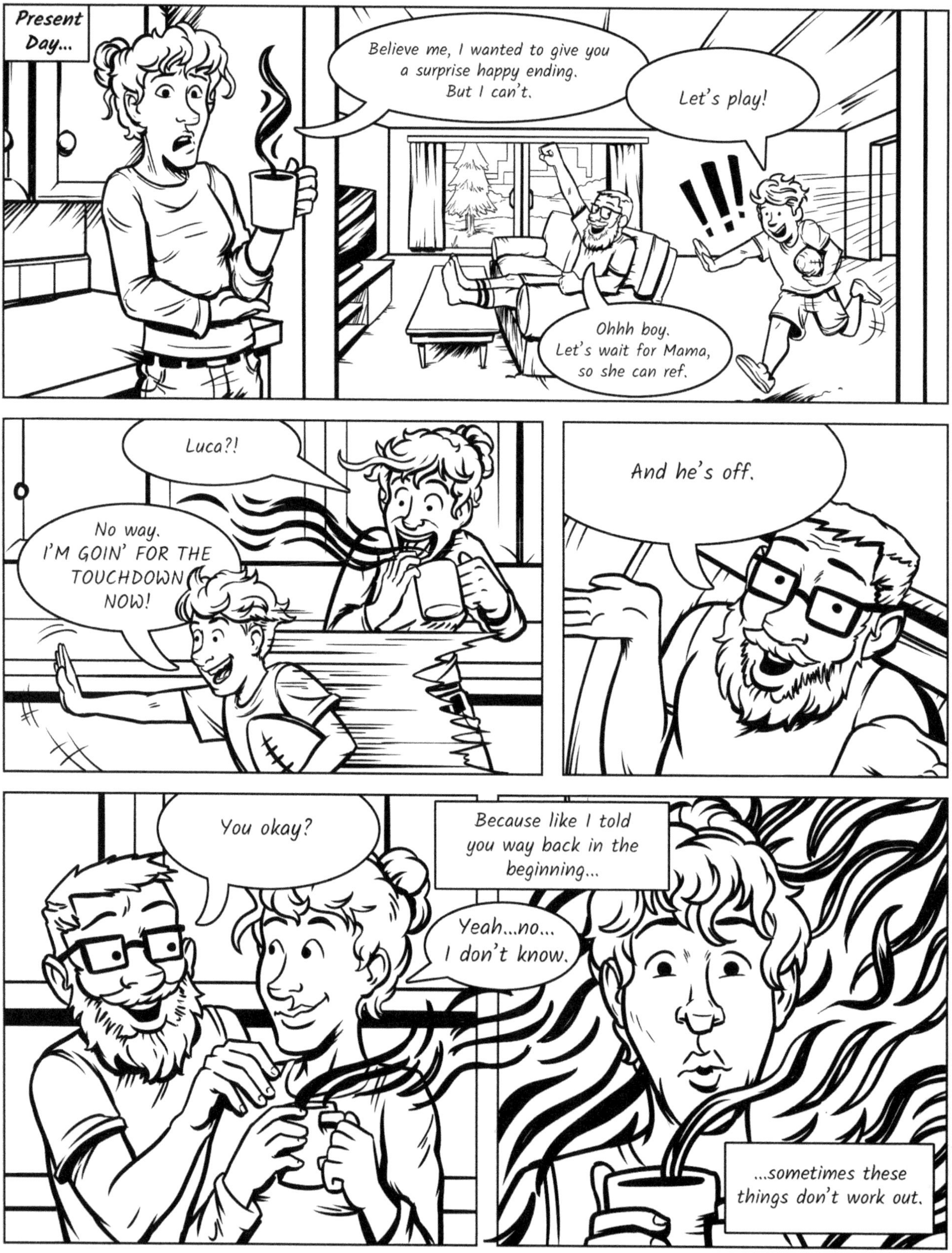
Present Day...
Believe me, I wanted to give you a surprise happy ending. But I can't.
Let's play!
!!!
Ohhh boy. Let's wait for Mama, so she can ref.
Luca?!
No way. I'M GOIN' FOR THE TOUCHDOWN NOW!
And he's off.
You okay?
Because like I told you way back in the beginning...
Yeah...no... I don't know.
...sometimes these things don't work out.

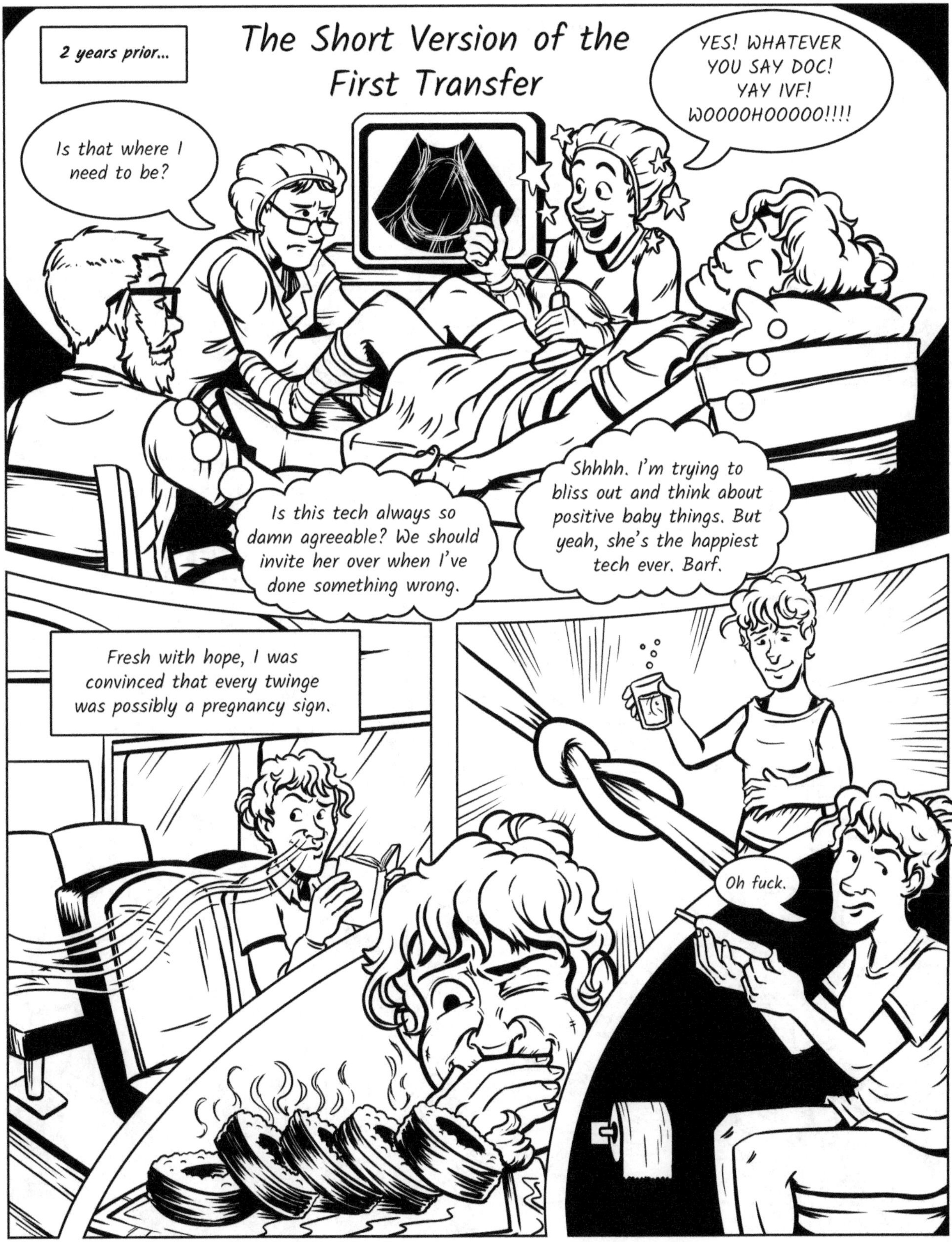
2 years prior...
The Short Version of the First Transfer
Is that where I need to be?
YES! WHATEVER YOU SAY DOC! YAY IVF! WOOOOHOOOOO!!!!
Is this tech always so damn agreeable? We should invite her over when I've done something wrong.
Shhhh. I'm trying to bliss out and think about positive baby things. But yeah, she's the happiest tech ever. Barf.
Fresh with hope, I was convinced that every twinge was possibly a pregnancy sign.
Oh fuck.

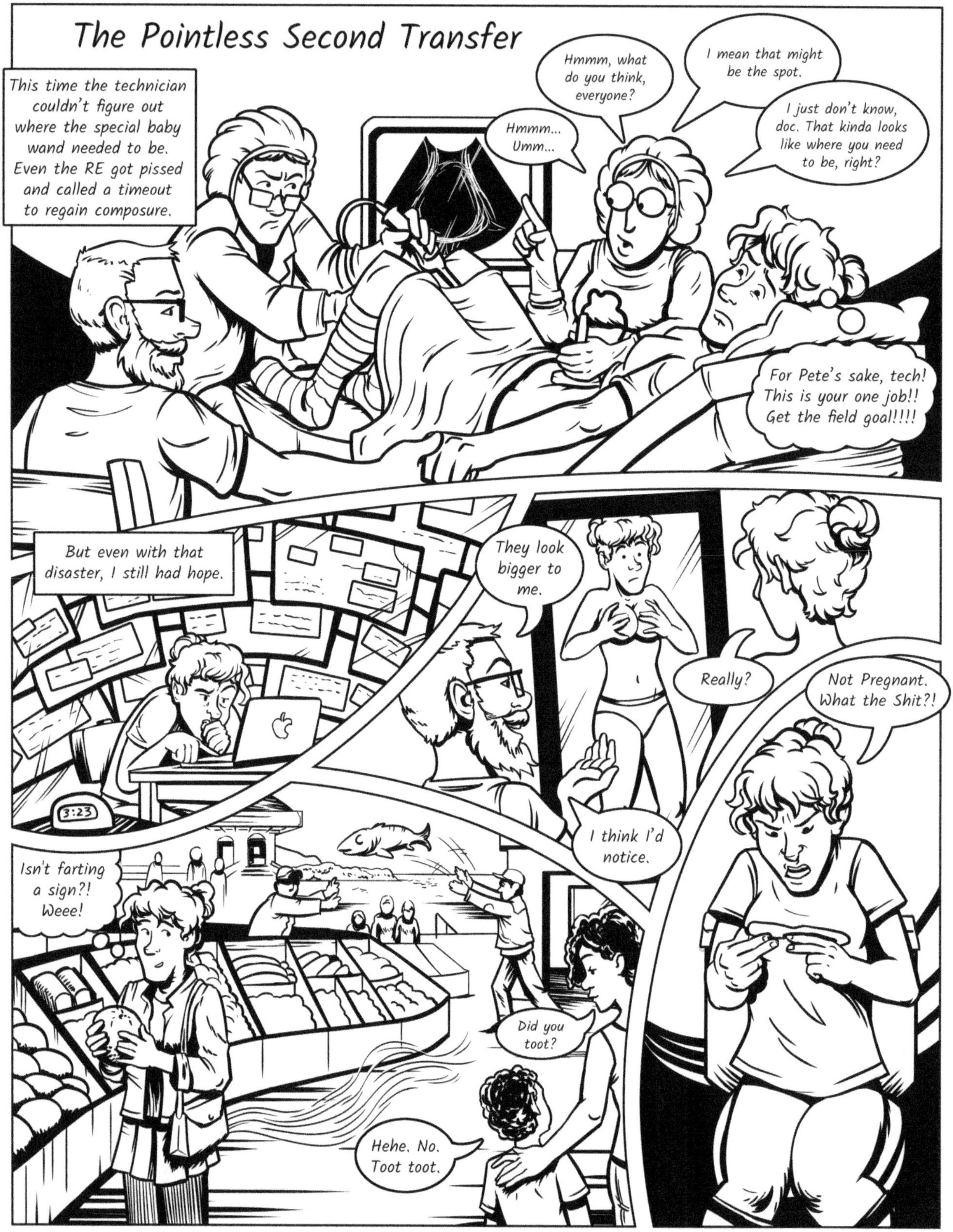
The Pointless Second Transfer
This time the technician couldn't figure out where the special baby wand needed to be. Even the RE got pissed and called a timeout to regain composure.
Hmmm... Umm...
Hmmm, what do you think, everyone?
I mean that might be the spot.
I just don't know, doc. That kinda looks like where you need to be, right?
For Pete's sake, tech! This is your one job!! Get the field goal!!!!
But even with that disaster, I still had hope.
3:23
They look bigger to me.
Really?
I think I'd notice.
Not Pregnant. What the Shit?!
Isn't farting a sign?! Weee!
Did you toot?
Hehe. No. Toot toot.

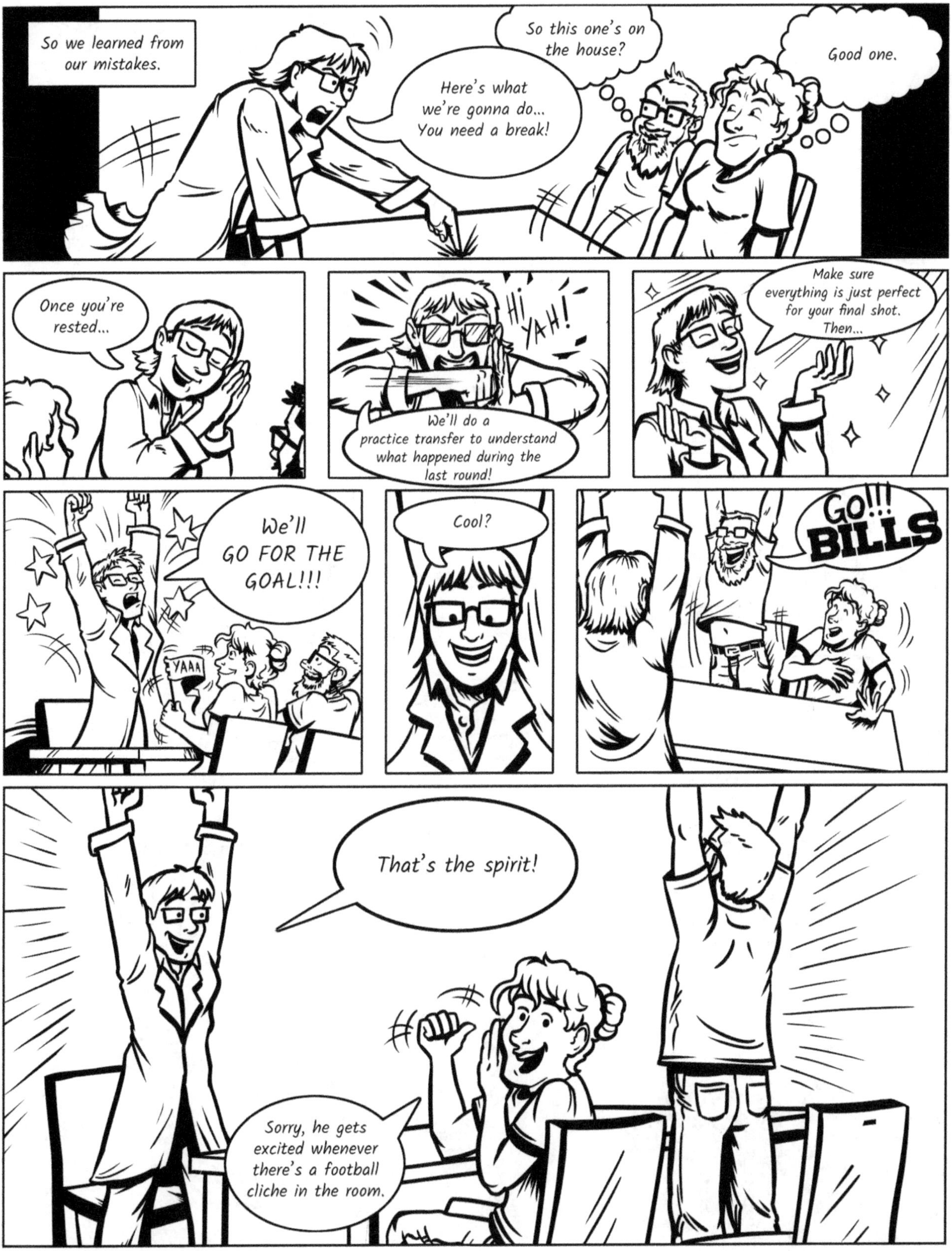
So we learned from our mistakes.
Here's what we're gonna do... You need a break!
So this one's on the house?
Good one.
Once you're rested...
HI YAH!
We'll do a practice transfer to understand what happened during the last round!
Make sure everything is just perfect for your final shot. Then...
We'll GO FOR THE GOAL!!!
YAAA
Cool?
GO!!! BILLS
That's the spirit!
Sorry, he gets excited whenever there's a football cliche in the room.

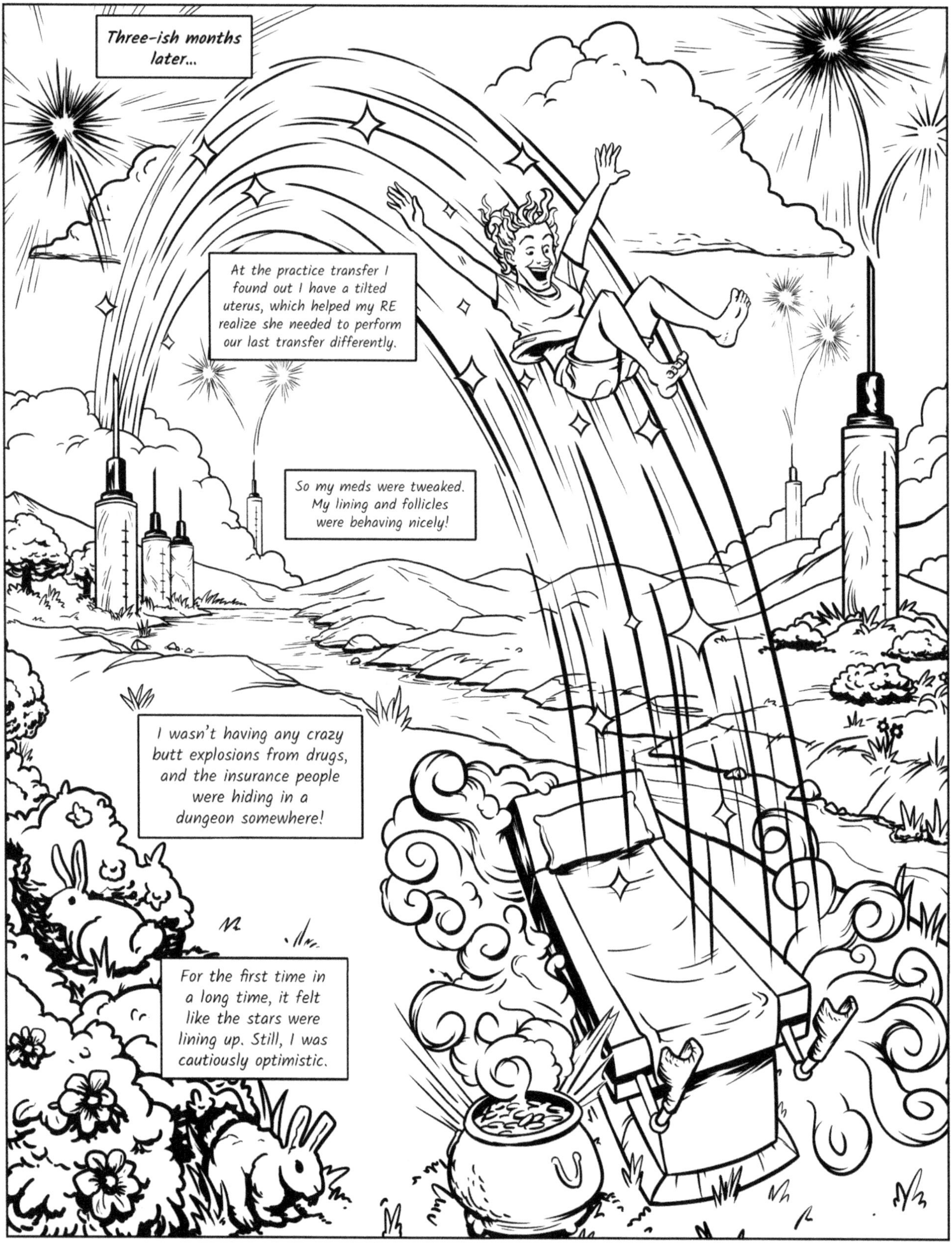
Three-ish months later...
At the practice transfer I found out I have a tilted uterus, which helped my RE realize she needed to perform our last transfer differently.
So my meds were tweaked. My lining and follicles were behaving nicely!
I wasn't having any crazy butt explosions from drugs, and the insurance people were hiding in a dungeon somewhere!
For the first time in a long time, it felt like the stars were lining up. Still, I was cautiously optimistic.

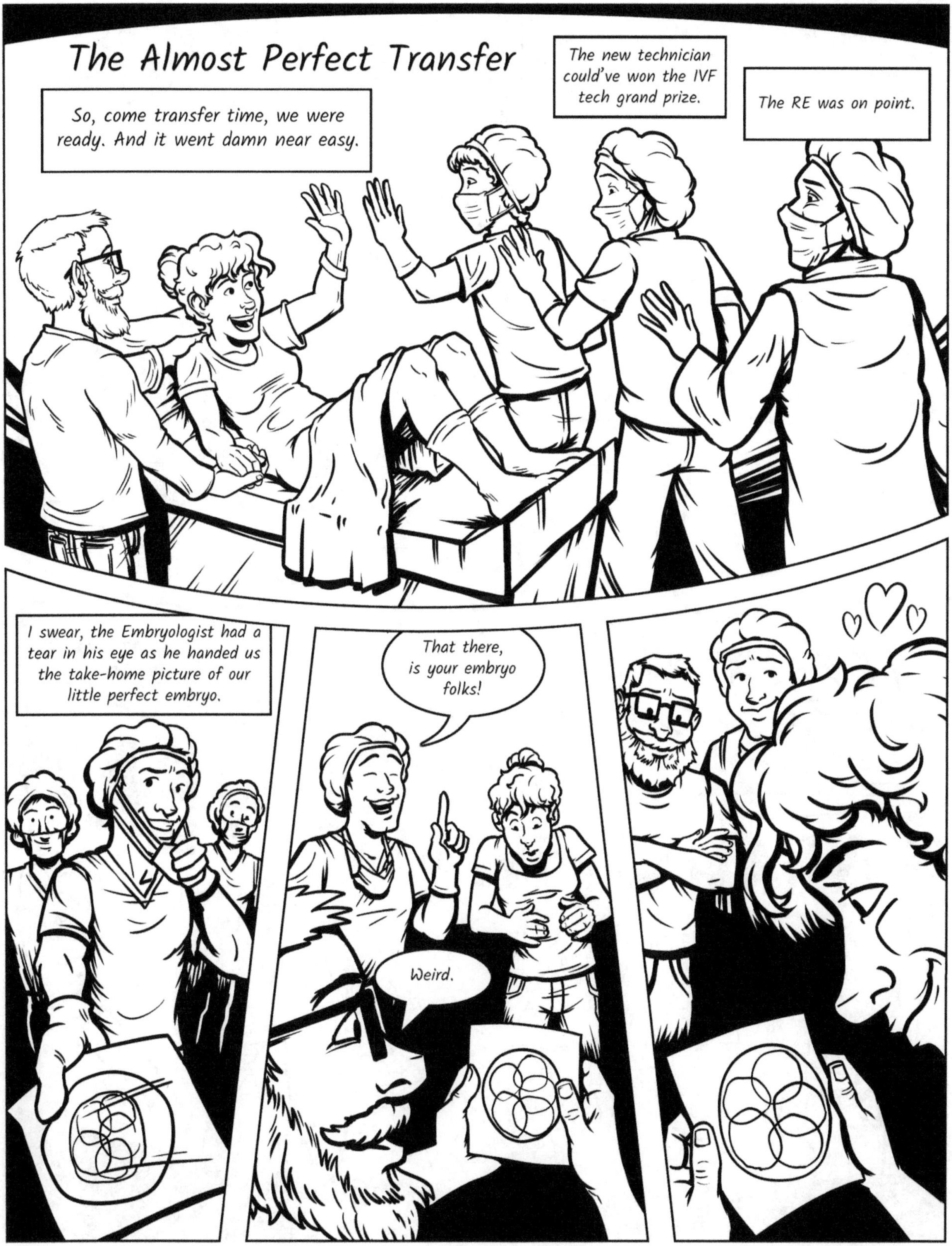
The Almost Perfect Transfer
So, come transfer time, we were ready. And it went damn near easy.
The new technician could've won the IVF tech grand prize.
The RE was on point.
I swear, the Embryologist had a tear in his eye as he handed us the take-home picture of our little perfect embryo.
That there, is your embryo folks!
Weird.

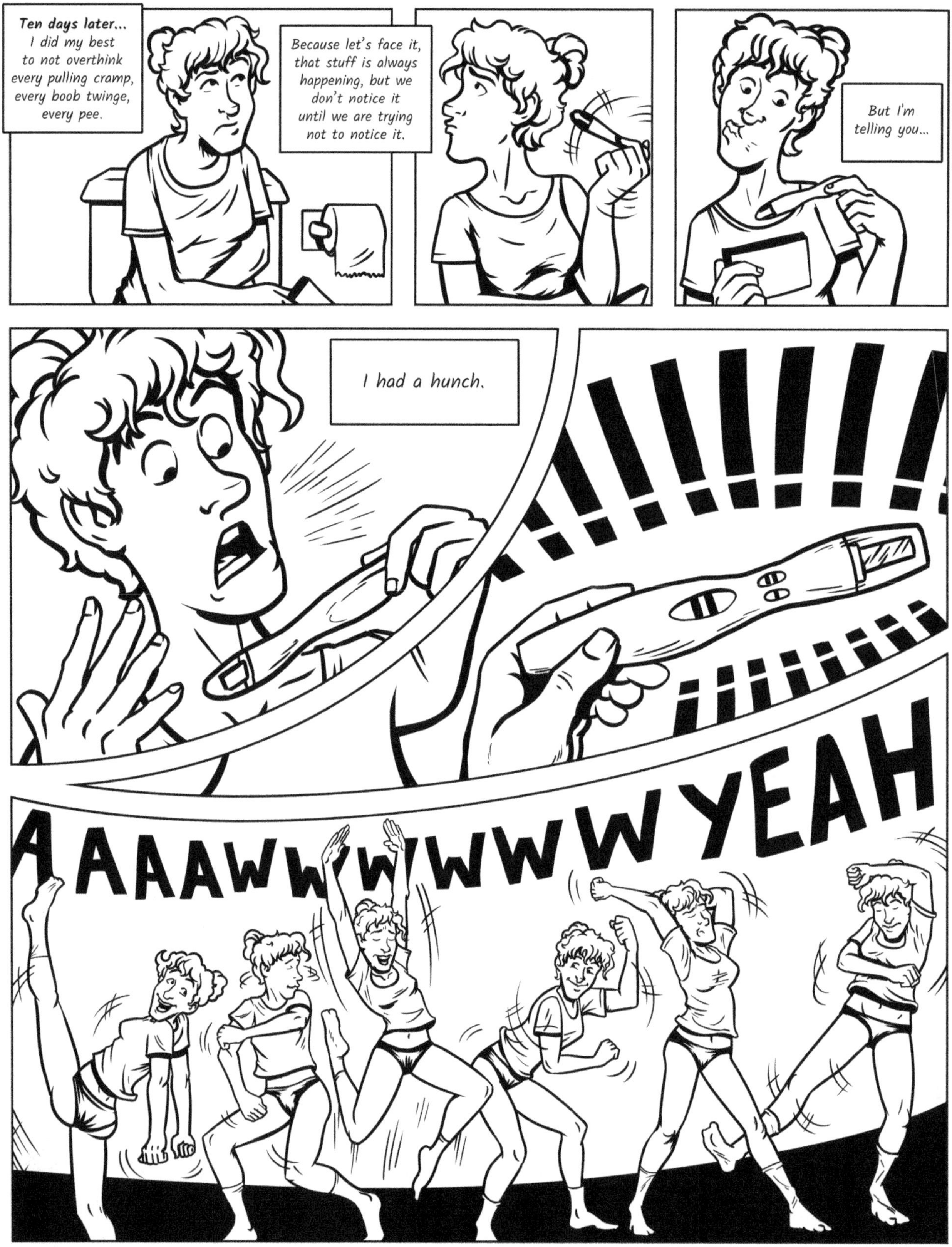
Ten days later... I did my best to not overthink every pulling cramp, every boob twinge, every pee.
Because let's face it, that stuff is always happening, but we don't notice it until we are trying not to notice it.
But I'm telling you...
I had a hunch.
!!!!!!!!
AAAAWWWWWWWYEAH

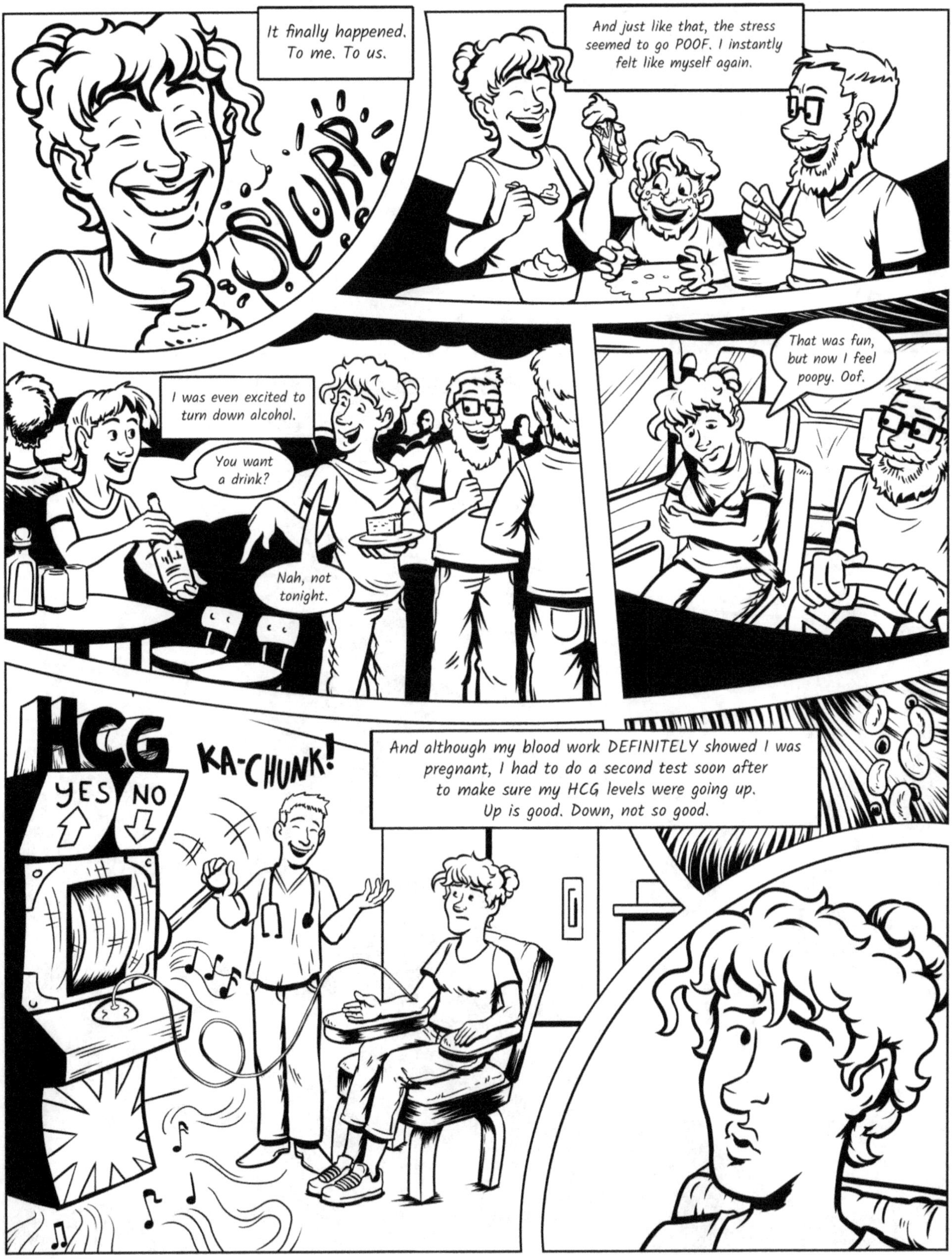
It finally happened. To me. To us.
SLURP
And just like that, the stress seemed to go POOF. I instantly felt like myself again.
I was even excited to turn down alcohol.
You want a drink?
Nah, not tonight.
That was fun, but now I feel poopy. Oof.
HCG
YES
NO
KA-CHUNK!
And although my blood work DEFINITELY showed I was pregnant, I had to do a second test soon after to make sure my HCG levels were going up. Up is good. Down, not so good.

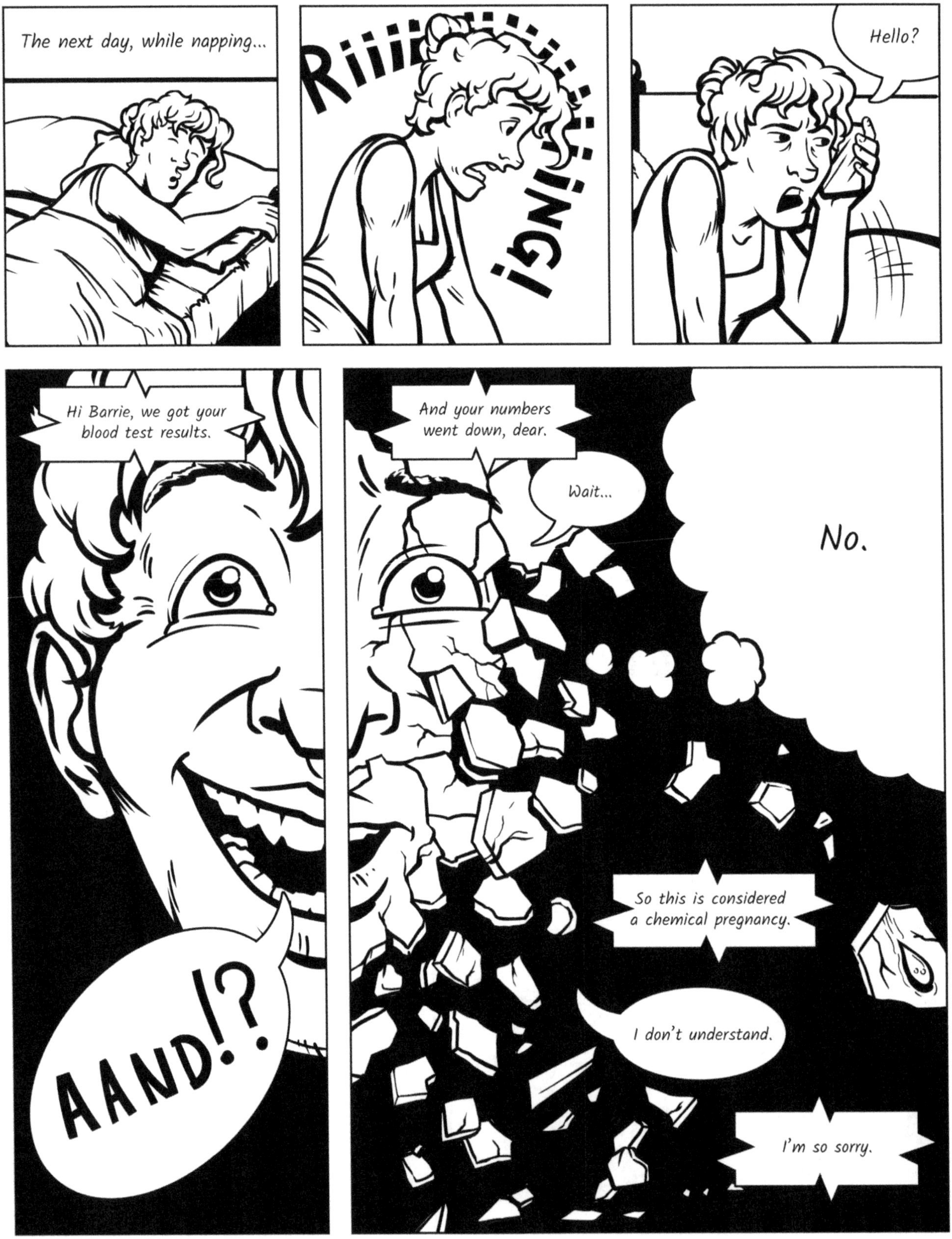
The next day, while napping...
RiiiiiiiiiiNG!
Hello?
Hi Barrie, we got your blood test results.
AAND!?
And your numbers went down, dear.
Wait...
No.
So this is considered a chemical pregnancy.
I don't understand.
I'm so sorry.

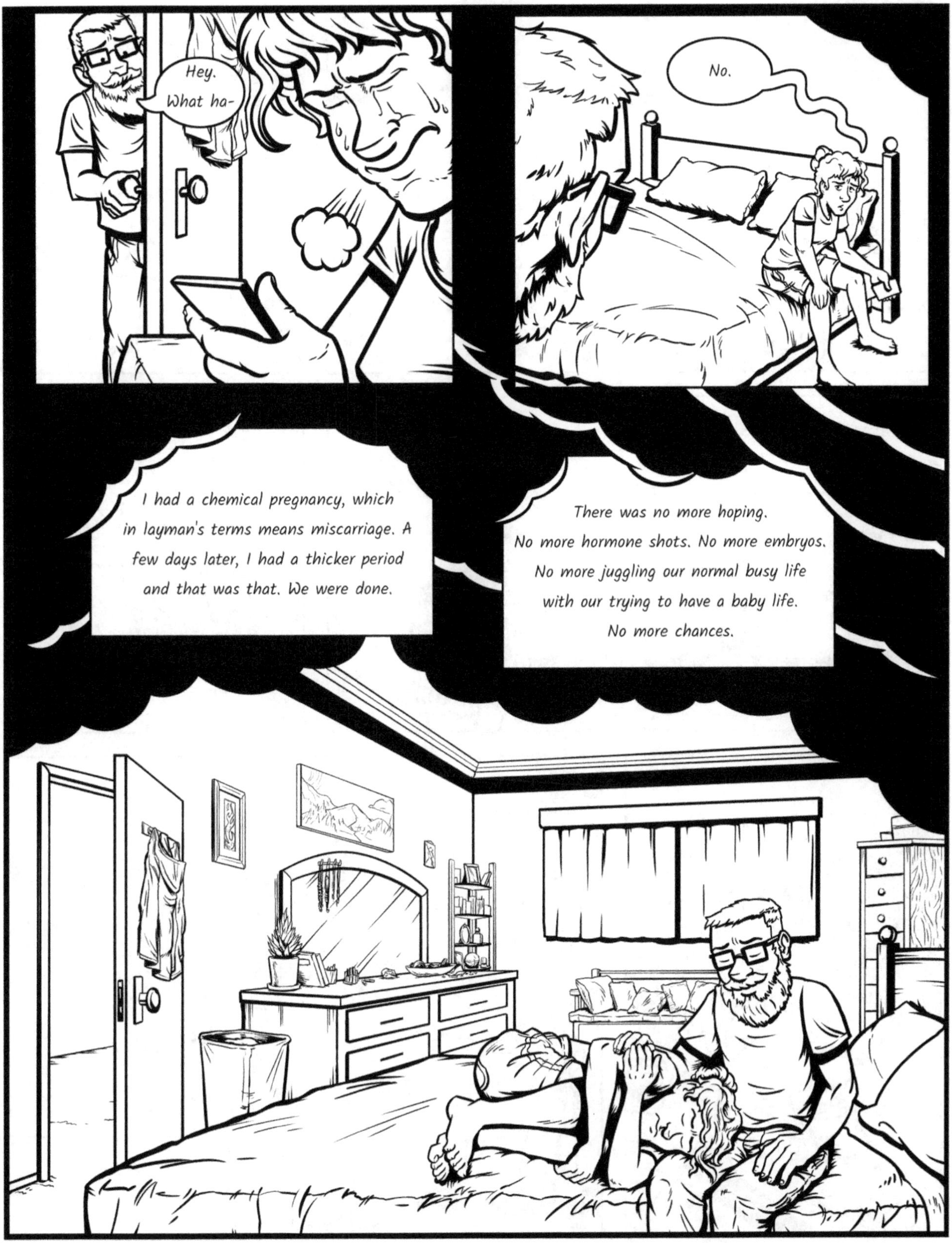
Hey.
What ha-
No.
I had a chemical pregnancy, which in layman's terms means miscarriage. A few days later, I had a thicker period and that was that. We were done.
There was no more hoping. No more hormone shots. No more embryos. No more juggling our normal busy life with our trying to have a baby life. No more chances.

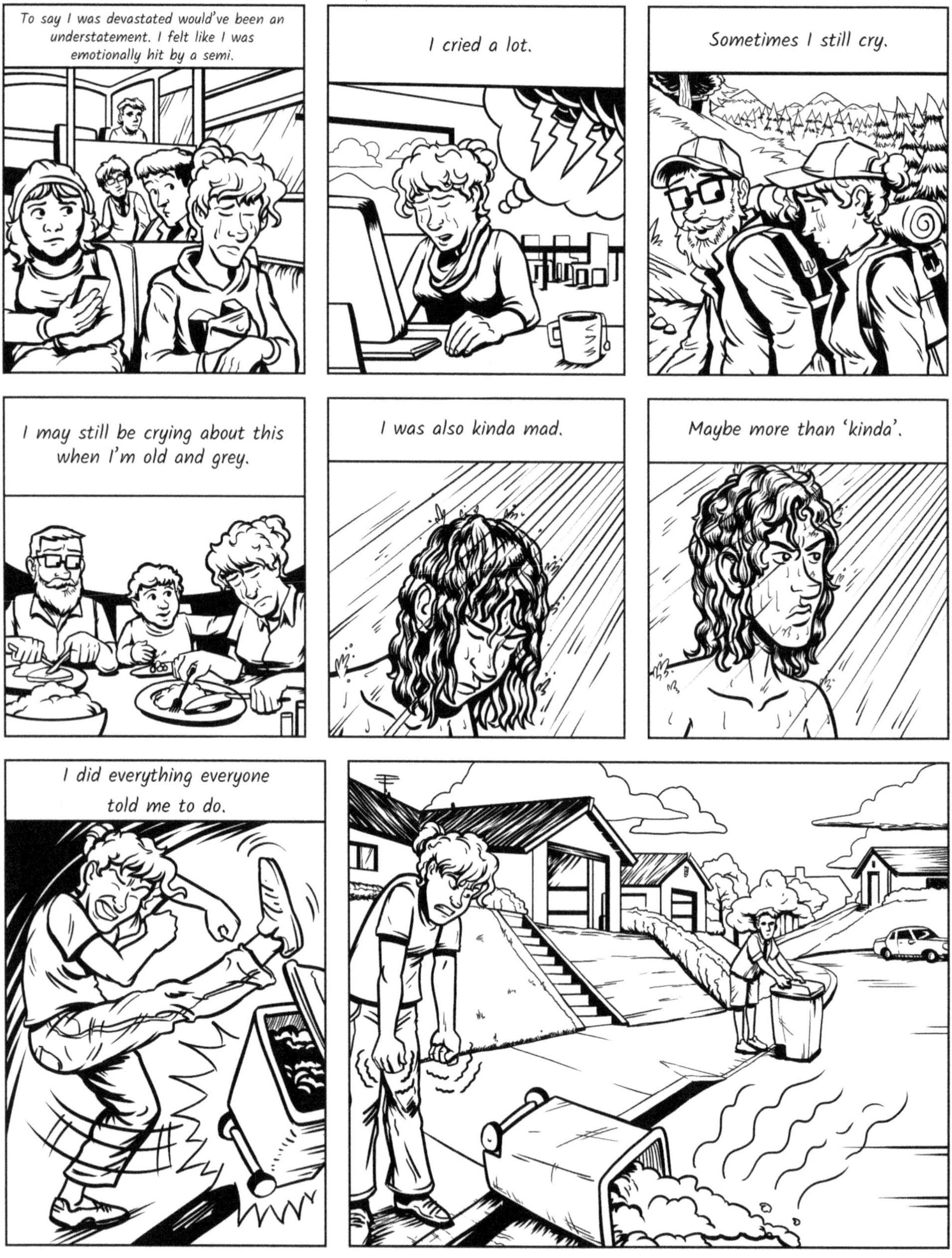
To say I was devastated would've been an understatement. I felt like I was emotionally hit by a semi.
I cried a lot.
Sometimes I still cry.
I may still be crying about this when I'm old and grey.
I was also kinda mad.
Maybe more than 'kinda'.
I did everything everyone told me to do.

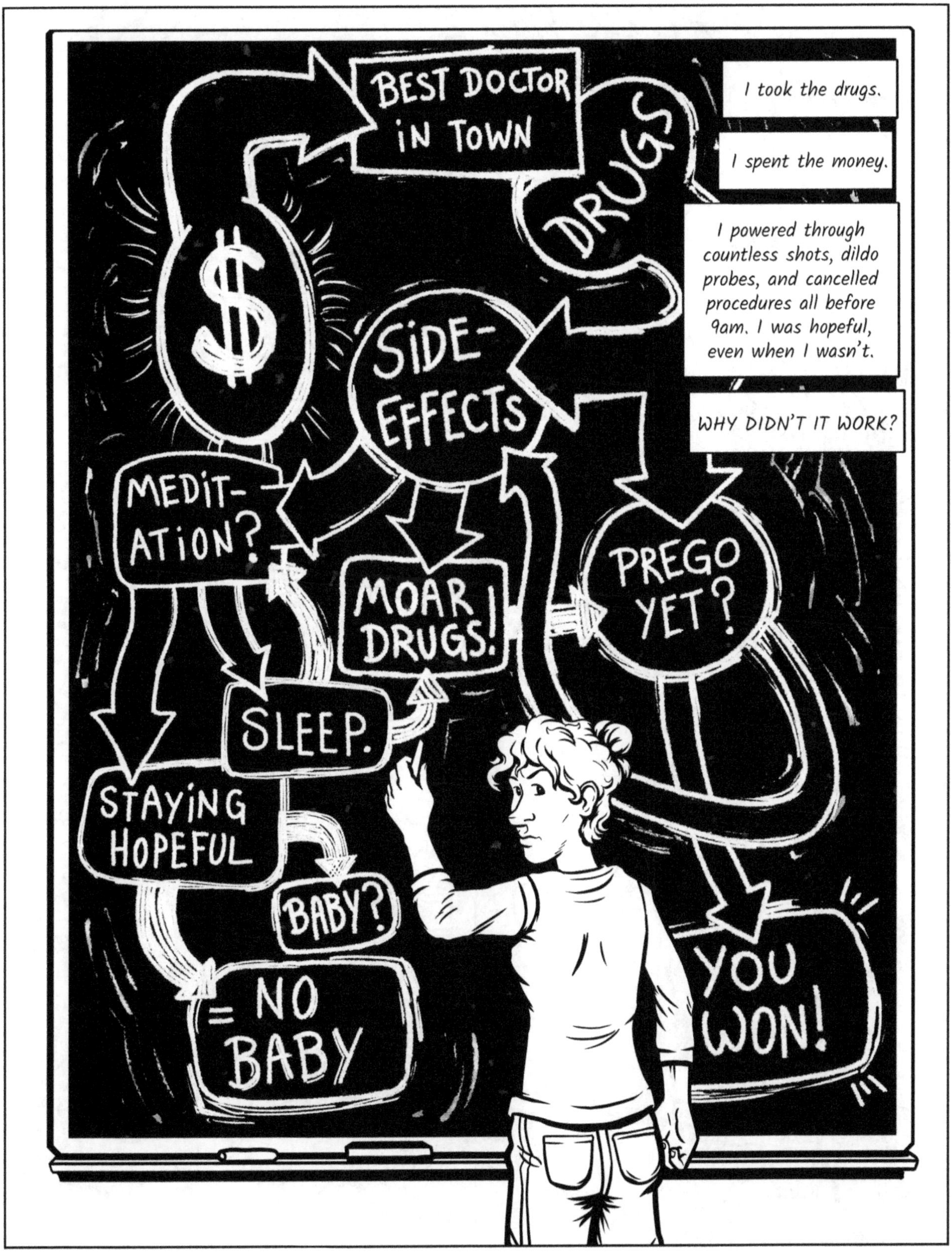
I took the drugs.
I spent the money.
I powered through countless shots, dildo probes, and cancelled procedures all before 9am. I was hopeful, even when I wasn't.
WHY DIDN'T IT WORK?
BEST DOCTOR IN TOWN
DRUGS
$
SIDE-EFFECTS
MEDIT-ATION?
MOAR DRUGS!
PREGO YET?
SLEEP.
STAYING HOPEFUL
BABY?
= NO BABY
YOU WON!

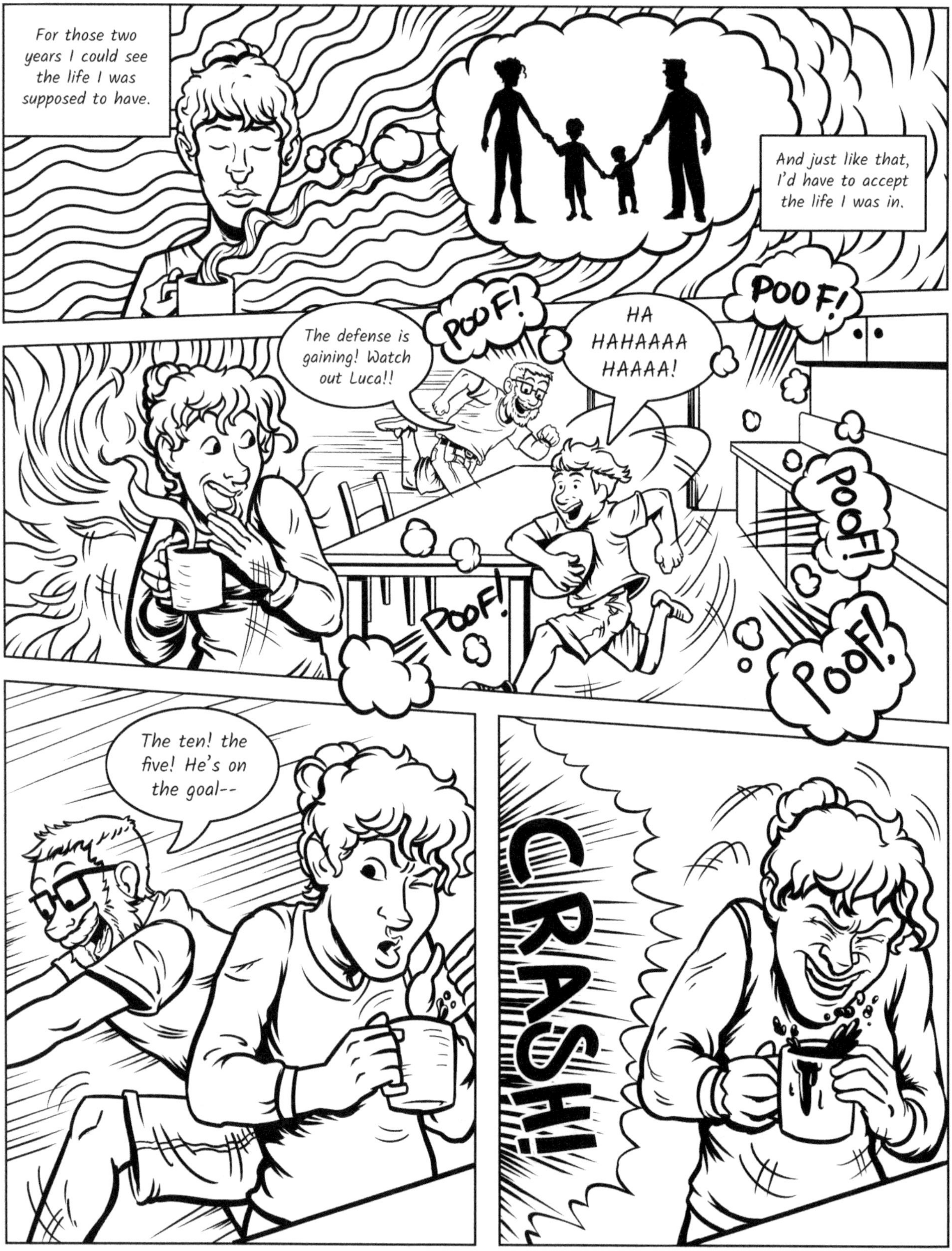
For those two years I could see the life I was supposed to have.
And just like that, I'd have to accept the life I was in.
The defense is gaining! Watch out Luca!!
POOF!
HA HAHAAAA HAAAA!
POOF!
POOF!
POOF!
POOF!
POOF!
The ten! the five! He's on the goal--
CRASH!!

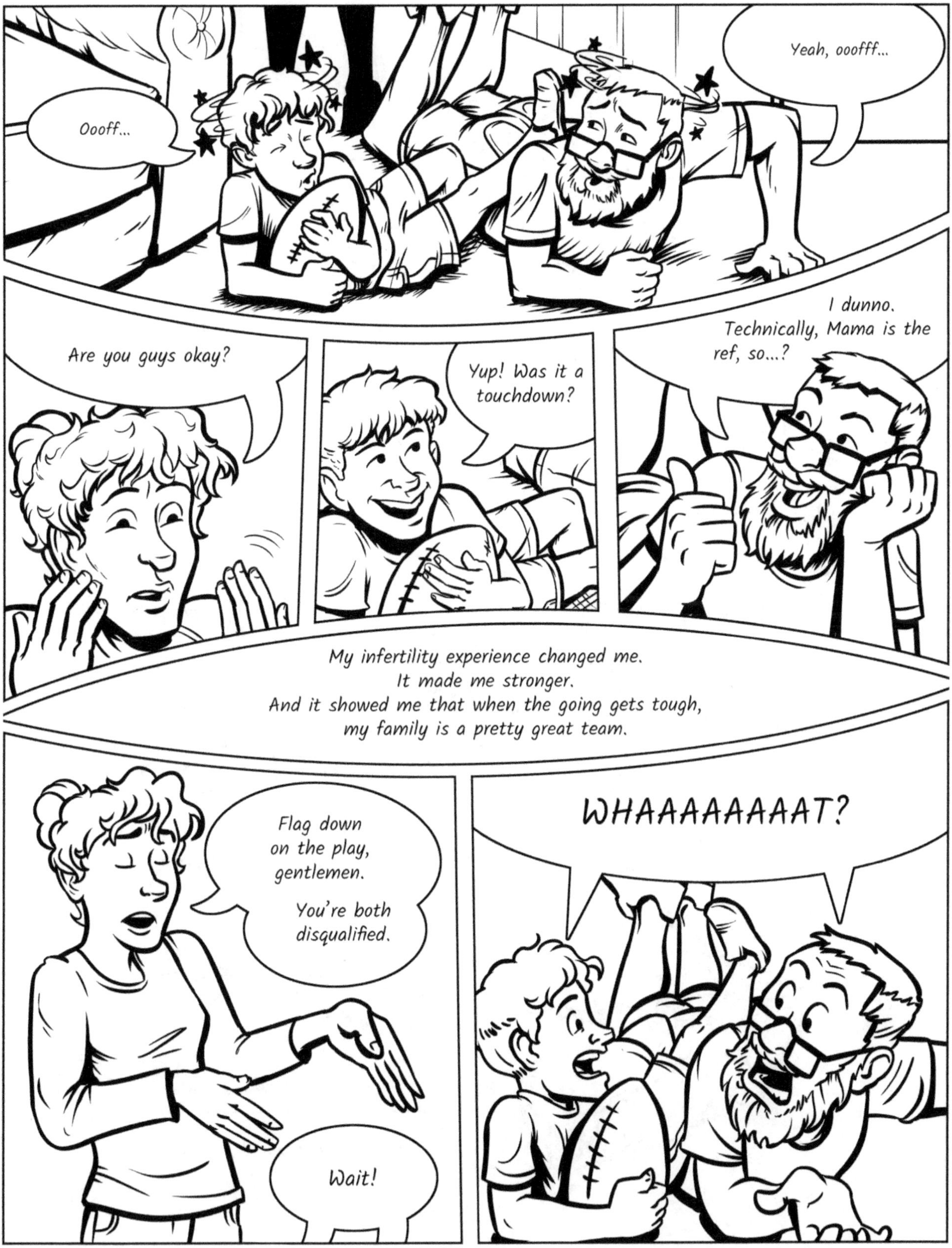
Oooff...
Yeah, ooofff...
Are you guys okay?
Yup! Was it a touchdown?
I dunno. Technically, Mama is the ref, so...?
My infertility experience changed me. It made me stronger. And it showed me that when the going gets tough, my family is a pretty great team.
Flag down on the play, gentlemen.
You're both disqualified.
Wait!
WHAAAAAAAAT?

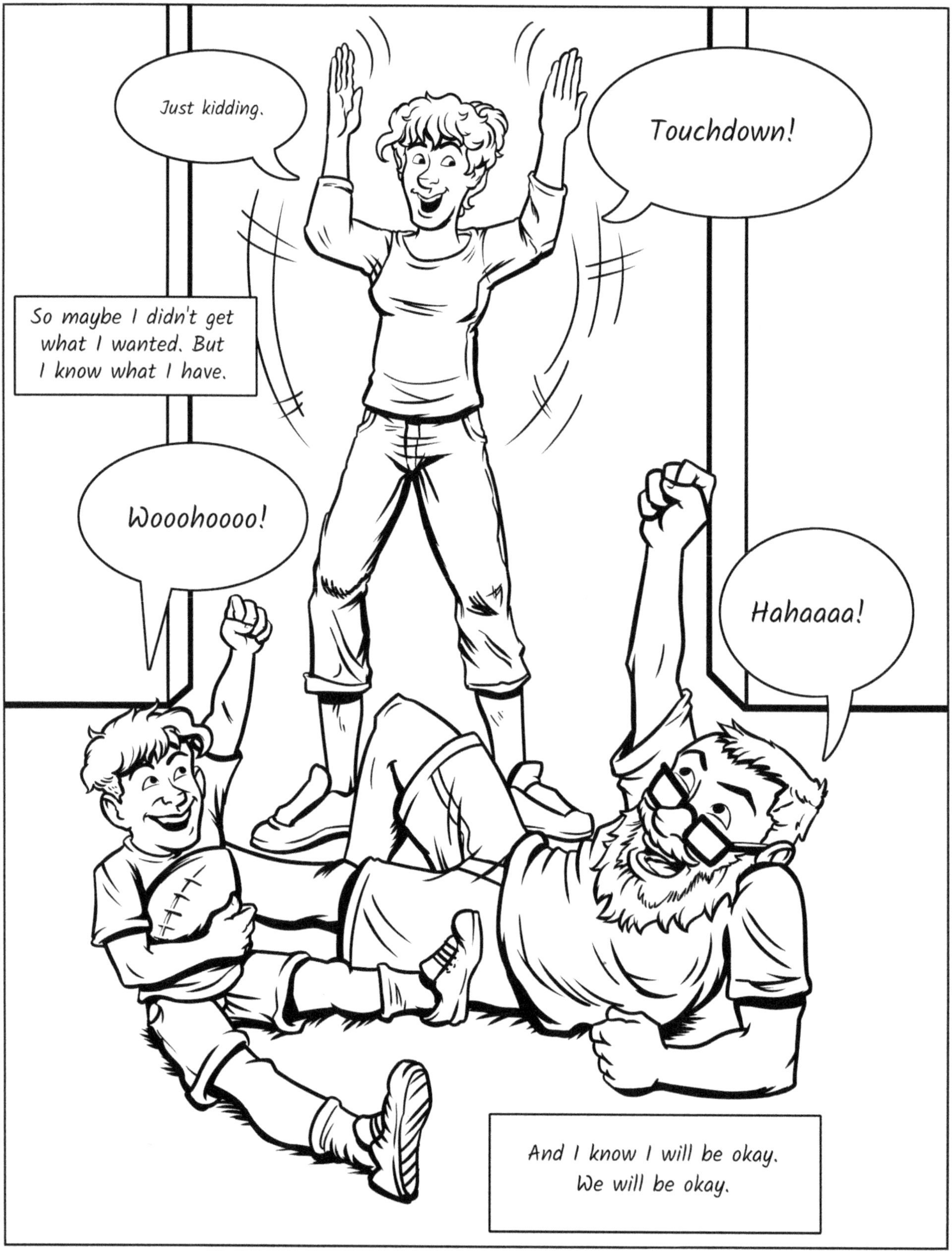
Just kidding.
Touchdown!
So maybe I didn't get what I wanted. But I know what I have.
Wooohoooo!
Hahaaaa!
And I know I will be okay. We will be okay.

Acknowledgements

Dan Louis Lane

I want to thank three people. Barrie, for making this project happen, and for inspiring me to do something new. Myself, for doing something I actually wanted to do for a change, and for surviving everything up to this point. Finally, to the random guy who abandoned his apartment and left behind the Microsoft Surface Pro (first generation) that I drew this thing on. Without his neglect I wouldn't have discovered that whatever I do next, I want to do it with ink on paper. Did I say three people? I meant five. My Mom and Dad for all the support.

Barrie Arliss

Thank you, Dan. You didn't know what you were getting into when I asked you to draw some pictures for me way back when. I couldn't have asked for a better illustrator to make my words come to life. To the people at PNWF, while we didn't get it right the second time, you brought me my son and, for that, I owe you the world. To my small family, my extended family, my friends, my community, and the total strangers who contributed to our GoFundMe-thank you for all your hugs, drinks, and cheerleading. To the fine people at Sou'wester, you gave me the space I desperately needed to write this book. To my editor, Maya, we may never actually talk on the phone, but you will always be my bosom buddy telling me to DO IT no matter what silly idea I pitch you. Dominic, thank you for always holding my hand at every damn appointment, rubbing my back when I cried, and for accepting our lot by being the greatest papa to our one and only. And of course, I couldn't leave this book without thanking Luca. You are my reason, my inspiration, my heart. Thank you for being everything I could have ever hoped for and yet never knew I needed until you arrived.

Creator Bios

Barrie Arliss makes her money as an advertising copywriter. When she's not working she's reading another self help book, obsessing about retiring early, dancing with her son, helping her community, or watching shows with her husband. She lives in Seattle.

agirlnamedbarrie.com

Dan Louis Lane is a Seattle cartoonist and storyteller. He worked as an animator and 3D artist before realizing his labor might be better directed toward driving a truck, moving stranger's furniture, and basking in the residual free time creating comics, paintings, and learning new forms of art and storytelling.

instagram.com/danlouislane

CPSIA information can be obtained
at www.ICGtesting.com
Printed in the USA
LVHW101830280120
645066LV00012B/570